SELECTIONS FROM THE WRITINGS OF THE PROMISED MESSIAH

(Urdu text with English Translation)

**Selections from the Writings of
The Promised Messiah**[as]
(Urdu text with English Translation)

First Published in UK in 1988
Reprinted in different countries several times

Editions Published in Qadian, India in 2012, 2013, 2015 .
Present Edition printed in Qadian, India in March 2016.

Copies: 6000

© Islam International Publications Ltd.

Published By:
Nazarat Nashr-o-Isha'at,
Sadr Anjuman Ahmadiyya Qadian,
Distt: Gurdaspur, Punjab-143516 (INDIA)

Printed in INDIA at Fazle Umar Printing Press Qadian.

ISBN: 978-81-7912-354-6

In celebration of the Centenary of the Worldwide Ahmadiyya Community.

This is a gift from those Ahmadi Muslims who, even in this age, are being persecuted and martyred merely because they love and proclaim the Unity of God. They are an embodiment of the spirit of Bilal.*

*Bilal (may God be pleased with him) was one of the companions of the Holy Prophet Muhammad, peace be upon him. Though he was subjected to extreme forms of torture due to his conversion to Islam, he was prepared to die rather than renounce his belief in the Unity of God.

CONTENTS

Preface	V
Allah the Exalted	1
The Divine Appreance	4
God's Treatment of People Loyal to Him	10
The Holy Prophet (Peace and blessings of Allah be upon him)	14
The Holy Quran	31
The Mission of the Promised Messiah (Peace be on him)	42
The Objective of Founding the Community	47
Admonitions	55
Thinking Ill of Others	59
Our Tenets	61
Angels	65
Revelation	68
The Soul	74
Life After Death	76
Sin	78
Salvation	80
Prayers	82
Jihad	83
Kindness unto Mankind	87
The True Nature of Gog and Magog	89
Season of Light	91
World Religions	95
The Future of Ahmadiyyat	97
Ultimate VIctory	99

PREFACE

The Ahmadiyya Muslim community, a worldwide Movement in Islam, was founded in 1889 at Qadian, India. Its Founder, Hadhrat Mirza Ghulam Ahmad, claimed to be the Promised Reformer whose advent was awaited under different names and titles by the adherents of various religions. The Hindus awaited Krishna; the Christians awaited the Messiah; the Buddhists awaited the Buddha and the Muslims awaited the Mahdi as well as the Messiah.

Under divine guidance, Hadhrat Mirza Ghulam Ahmad made the revolutionary disclosure that there was to appear only one such Reformer representing all these Promised Ones, whose mission was to ultimately bring mankind into the fold of one universal religion. He also maintained that the Promised Reformer was to appear, not in an independent capacity, but as a subordinate to the Holy Prophet of Islam, Hadhrat Muhammad Mustafa, peace and blessings of Allah be upon him. He believed Islam to be the final and complete code of life for all mankind and hence his claim that the awaited Reformer had to appear in Islam as a subordinate prophet to Hadhrat Muhammad Mustafa, peace be upon him. His advent, he declared, would finally usher a golden era of one universal religion which for ages man had dreamt of and yearned for.

In 1889, he was commissioned by Allah to lay the foundation of a community which would pursue the goals and objectives of his advent. And hence on the 23rd of March, 1889, by accepting the Oath of Allegiance, he formally initiated the Ahmadiyya Muslim Community at Ludhiana, a small town in Punjab, India.

On partition of India, the Headquarters of the Ahmadiyya Muslim Community were shifted to Pakistan where the Community built a small town, Rabwah, to be used as its

Headquarters.

More than a century has lapsed since Hadhrat Mirza Ghulam Ahmad of claimed to be an apostle sent by Allah Almighty. Ironically, since the initiation of the Ahmadiyya Muslim Community, there have been many hostile movements launched against the Community. The most well known among these are the anti Ahmadiyya movements of 1953, 1974 and 1984. The 1984 movement, however, was launched with the full support of General Ziaul Haq's Military Junta in Pakistan which promulgated an Ordinance restricting the basic and fundamental human rights of the Ahmadiyya Muslim Community in Pakistan. As a result of this ordinance thousands of Ahmadi Muslims have been subjected to the most terrible persecution which varies from imprisonment to physical torture and also genocide.

Yet despite intense controversy and excessive hostility, the Ahmadiyya Muslim Community has continued to make rapid progress in all parts of the world and it continues to march forward as the true Voice of Islam and although it has had to make immense sacrifices, every hostile movement against the community has been frustrated by the grace of Allah.

In fact, as a result of the hostilities, Ahmadi Muslims have reacted with immense resolve and a spirit of rejuvenation which has increased the Community's pace of progress many times over.

This selection from the writings of Hadhrat Mirza Ghulam Ahmad, the promised Messiah and Mahdi, peace be on him, was made by Hadhrat Mirza Tahir Ahmad, Khalifatul Masih IV,may Allah have mercy on him, the Supreme Head of the Worldwide Ahmadiyya Muslim Community from 1982 to 2003.

This selection covers the following important subjects.:-
1. Allah the Exalted   2. The Divine Appearance
3. God's Treatment of People Loyal to Him
4. The Holy Prophet   5. The Holy Quran
6. The Mission of the Promised Messiah
7.The Objective of Founding the Community

8.Admonitions   9. Thinking Ill of Others

10.Our Tenets   11.Angels

12. Revelation   13.The Soul

14.Life After Death   15.Sin

16.Salvation   17.Prayers

18.Jihad   19. Kindness Unto Mankind

20.The True Nature of Gog and Magog

21.Season of Light   22.World Religions

23.The Future of Ahmadiyyat   24.Ultimate Victory

This selection from the Writings of the Promised Messiah, peace be upon him, was a part of the program commemorating the Centenary Celebrations of the Ahmadiyya Muslim Community. It contains a few selected passages from his writings and these should shed some light on the various aspects of the Community's beliefs and philosophy.

We hope that the reader would find this study, through a miniature window to more than 80 books written by the Promised Messiah, not only informative but also illuminating and inspiring. For more information please visit www.alislam.org

Naseer Ahmad Qamar
Additional Wakil ul Isha'at London
December 2011

ALLAH THE EXALTED

1۔ ''ہمارا بہشت ہمارا خدا ہے۔ ہماری اعلیٰ لذّات ہمارے خدا میں ہیں کیونکہ ہم نے اس کو دیکھا اور ہر ایک خوبصورتی اس میں پائی۔ یہ دولت لینے کے لائق ہے اگرچہ جان دینے سے ملے اور یہ لعل خریدنے کے لائق ہے اگرچہ تمام وجود کھونے سے حاصل ہو۔ اے محرومو! اس چشمہ کی طرف دوڑو کہ وہ تمہیں سیراب کرے گا۔ یہ زندگی کا چشمہ ہے جو تمہیں بچائے گا۔ میں کیا کروں اور کس طرح اس خوشخبری کو دلوں میں بٹھا دوں۔ کس دَف سے مَیں بازاروں میں منادی کروں کہ تمہارا یہ خدا ہے تا لوگ سن لیں اور کس دوا سے مَیں علاج کروں تا سننے کے لئے لوگوں کے کان کھلیں۔ اگر تم خدا کے ہو جاؤ گے تو یقیناً سمجھو کہ خدا تمہارا ہی ہے''۔

(کشتی نوح، روحانی خزائن جلد 19 صفحہ 21,22)

1- Our paradise is in our God. Our highest delight is in our God for we have seen Him and have found every beauty in Him. This wealth is worth procuring though one may have to lay down one's life to procure it. This ruby is worth purchasing though one may have to lose one's self to acquire it. 0 ye, who are bereft, run to this fountain and it will satiate your thirst. It is the fountain of life that will save you. What shall I do, and by what drum shall I make the announcement that this is your God, so that people might hear? What remedy shall I apply to their ears so that they should listen. If you belong to Allah, rest assured that Allah will indeed belong to you.

(Kishti Nuh; Roohani Khaza'in, Vol. 19, pp. 21-22)

2۔ ''اے سننے والو سنو! کہ خدا تم سے کیا چاہتا ہے۔ بس یہی کہ تم اُسی کے ہو جاؤ۔ اُس

کے ساتھ کسی کو بھی شریک نہ کرو۔ نہ آسمان میں نہ زمین میں۔ ہمارا خدا وہ خدا ہے جو اب بھی زندہ ہے جیسا کہ پہلے زندہ تھا اور اب بھی وہ بولتا ہے جیسا کہ وہ پہلے بولتا تھا اور اب بھی وہ سنتا ہے جیسا کہ پہلے سنتا تھا۔ یہ خیال خام ہے کہ اس زمانہ میں وہ سنتا تو ہے مگر بولتا نہیں۔ بلکہ وہ سنتا ہے اور بولتا بھی ہے۔ اس کی تمام صفات ازلی ابدی ہیں۔ کوئی صفت بھی معطل نہیں اور نہ کبھی ہوگی۔ وہ وہی واحد لاشریک ہے جس کا کوئی بیٹا نہیں اور جس کی کوئی بیوی نہیں۔ وہ وہی بے مثل ہے جس کا کوئی ثانی نہیں ۔۔۔۔۔۔۔۔۔۔ جس کا کوئی ہم صفات نہیں اور جس کی کوئی طاقت کم نہیں۔ وہ قریب ہے باوجود دُور ہونے کے اور دُور ہے باوجود نزدیک ہونے کے ۔۔۔۔۔۔۔۔۔۔ وہ سب سے اوپر ہے مگر نہیں کہہ سکتے کہ اس کے نیچے کوئی اور بھی ہے۔ اور وہ عرش پر ہے مگر نہیں کہہ سکتے کہ زمین پر نہیں۔ وہ مجمع ہے تمام صفات کاملہ کا اور مظہر ہے تمام محامدِ حقّہ کا اور سر چشمہ ہے تمام خوبیوں کا۔ اور جامع ہے تمام طاقتوں کا۔ اور مبدء ہے تمام فیضوں کا۔ اور مرجع ہے ہر ایک شَے کا۔ اور مالک ہے ہر ایک مُلک کا۔ اور متّصف ہے ہر ایک کمال سے۔ اور منزّہ ہے ہر ایک عیب اور ضُعف سے۔ اور مخصوص ہے اِس امر میں کہ زمین والے اور آسمان والے اُسی کی عبادت کریں''۔

(الوصیّت، روحانی خزائن جلد 20 صفحہ 309-310)

2- Hearken ye who have ears to hear: What is it that Allah requires of you? Only this that you should become His alone and set up no equal with Him, neither on this earth nor in heaven. Our God is the One Who is alive today as much as He ever was. Likewise, He speaks today as He did in the past; He hears as He used to hear. To think that He only listens but does not speak in this age is a vain belief. Indeed, He both hears and speaks. All His attributes are eternal and everlasting. None of His attributes were ever suspended, nor will they ever be. He is the same Unique

Being Who has no associate. He has neither son nor wife, and He is the same Eternal Being Who is peerless, and there is none like unto Him........ There is no one similar to Him in His attributes; none of His powers ever wane. He is near, yet far; distant, yet close........ He is the Highest of the high, yet it cannot be said that there is anyone below Him (farther than He). He is in Heaven, but it cannot be said that He is not on earth. He combines in Himself all the most perfect attributes and manifests the virtues which are truly worthy of praise. He is the Fountainhead of all excellence. He is the All Powerful. Everything good originates from Him and to Him all things return. All possessions belong to Him, and in Him all excellences combine. He is free from blemish, without weakness. He is Unique in His right to be worshipped by all who dwell on the earth or belong to heaven.

(Al Wasiyyat: Roohani Khaza'in, Vol. 20, pp. 309,310)

THE DIVINE APPEARANCE

۳۔ جس کو شبہات سے نجات نہیں اس کو عذاب سے بھی نجات نہیں۔ جو شخص اس دنیا میں خدا کے دیکھنے سے بے نصیب ہے وہ قیامت میں بھی تاریکی میں گرے گا۔ خدا کا قول ہے کہ مَنْ کَانَ فِیْ ھٰذِہٖ اَعْمٰی فَھُوَ فِی الْاٰخِرَۃِ اَعْمٰی ۔ (بنی اسرائیل:73)

(کتاب البریہ، روحانی خزائن جلد 13 صفحہ 65)

3- The one who is not rid of doubt is not secure from punishment either. The one who is ill fated to be deprived of seeing God in this world will also have the pit of darkness as his fate in the Hereafter. God says: "But he who is blind in this world will be blind in the Hereafter."   (Bani Israel 17:73)

(*Kitabul Bariyya: Roohani Khaza'in,, Vol. 13, p. 65*)

۴۔ ''میں سچ سچ کہتا ہوں کہ اگر روحوں میں سچی تلاش پیدا ہوا اور دلوں میں سچی پیاس لگ جائے تو لوگ اس طریق کو ڈھونڈیں اور اُس راہ کی تلاش میں لگیں۔ مگر یہ راہ کس طریق سے کھلے گی اور حجاب کس دوا سے اٹھے گا۔ مَیں سب طالبوں کو یقین دلاتا ہوں کہ صرف اسلام ہی ہے جو اس راہ کی خوشخبری دیتا ہے۔ اور دوسری قومیں تو خدا کے الہام پر مدت سے مُہر لگا چکی ہیں۔ سو یقیناً سمجھو کہ یہ خدا کی طرف سے مُہر نہیں بلکہ محرومی کی وجہ سے انسان ایک حیلہ پیدا کر لیتا ہے۔ اور یقیناً یہ سمجھو کہ جس طرح یہ ممکن نہیں کہ ہم بغیر آنکھوں کے دیکھ سکیں یا بغیر کانوں کے سن سکیں یا بغیر زبان کے بول سکیں اِسی طرح یہ بھی ممکن نہیں کہ بغیر قرآن کے اُس پیارے محبوب کا منہ دیکھ سکیں۔ مَیں جوان تھا۔ اب بوڑھا ہوا مگر مَیں نے کوئی نہ پایا جس نے بغیر اس پاک چشمہ کے اس کھلی کھلی

4- I speak the truth and nothing but the truth. If souls are endowed with a sincere desire to search, and hearts become thirsty after knowledge, then mankind will yearn to discover that Path and that Way. But how can one have access to that Path and how can the veil be lifted? I assure all those who seek that it is Islam alone which gives the glad tidings of the Way. The other faiths have long since put an end to the institution of revelation from God. So rest assured that it is not God Who has brought revelation to a close. But it is man, who, to justify his deprivation, seeks shelter in this false excuse. Fully realize that as it is not possible to see without eyes or to hear without ears or to speak without tongues, so also it is not possible to set eyes on our Beloved God without the aid of the Holy Quran. I was young once. Now I am old. But I found none who, without having access to this pure fountainhead, the Quran, drank out of the cup of such manifest and clear guidance.

(Islami Usul ki Philosophy: Roohani Khaza'in Vol. 10, pp.442-443)

5۔ کس قدر ظاہر ہے نور اُس مبدء الانوار کا

بن رہا ہے سارا عالم آئینہ اَبصار کا

چاند کو کل دیکھ کر میں سخت بے کل ہو گیا

کیونکہ کچھ کچھ تھا نشاں اس میں جمال یار کا

اُس بہار حسن کا دل میں ہمارے جوش ہے

مت کرو کچھ ذکر ہم سے ترک یا تاتار کا

ہے عجب جلوہ تری قدرت کا پیارے ہر طرف

جس طرف دیکھیں وہی رہ ہے ترے دیدار کا

چشمۂ خورشید میں موجیں تری مشہود ہیں

ہر ستارے میں تماشا ہے تری چمکار کا

تو نے خود روحوں پہ اپنے ہاتھ سے چھڑکا نمک

اس سے ہے شور محبت عاشقانِ زار کا

کیا عجب تو نے ہر ایک ذرہ میں رکھے ہیں خواص

کون پڑھ سکتا ہے سارا دفتر ان اسرار کا

تیری قدرت کا کوئی بھی انتہا پاتا نہیں

کس سے کھل سکتا ہے پیچ اس عقدۂ دشوار کا

خوبرویوں میں ملاحت ہے ترے اس حسن کی

ہر گل و گلشن میں ہے رنگ اس تری گلزار کا

چشمِ مستِ ہر حسیں ہر دم دکھاتی ہے تجھے

ہاتھ ہے تیری طرف ہر گیسوئے خمدار کا

(سُرمہ چشم آریہ، روحانی خزائن جلد 2 صفحہ 52)

5- Lo! How manifest is the Light of God,
   Who is the ultimate Source of all light;
   The whole universe is turning into
   a reflecting mirror;
   for the eyes to perceive Him.

   Last night while watching the moon,
   I became so agitated.
   In the beauty of the moon
   were the traces of the beauty
   of my Beloved.

Under the influence
of that consummate Beauty;
my heart is in a state of turmoil;
mention not to me the comeliness
of the Turk or the Tartar.

O my Beloved!
How wonderfully is Thy
creative power Manifested everywhere;
Whichever way I look I find
every road leading to Thy Presence.

In the fountain of the sun,
the tides of Thy power are witnessed;
Every star is twinkling with Thy Glory.

With Thy own hand Thou hast
sprinkled salt over smarting hearts;
Which results into
agonized cries of the pining lovers.

No one can comprehend
the ultimate design of Thy Creation;
Who can disentangle
the web of this baffling riddle?

It is Thy charm which is
the essence of every beauty;
Every flower that blossoms forth
borrows its color
from the splendor of Thy attributes.

The mellow intoxicating eyes of all

who are endowed with beauty;
Remind one of Thee every moment.
To Thy direction is turned
the pointing finger
of every curly lock.

With what mysterious qualities,
Thou hast endowed every particle;
Who can read through the voluminous,
accounts of these mysteries?
(Surma Chashm Arya: Roohani Khaza'in, Vol. 2, p.52; from the poem: 'A Hymn to God'.)

۔6   توحید ایک نور ہے جو آفاقی وانفسی معبودوں کی نفی کے بعد دل میں پیدا ہوتا ہے اور وجود کے ذرّہ ذرّہ میں سرایت کر جاتا ہے۔ پس وہ بُجز خدا اور اُس کے رسول کے ذریعہ کے محض اپنی طاقت سے کیونکر حاصل ہوسکتا ہے۔ انسان کا فقط یہ کام ہے کہ اپنی خودی پر موت وارد کرے۔ اس شیطانی نخوت کو چھوڑ دے کہ مَیں علوم میں پرورش یافتہ ہوں اور ایک جاہل کی طرح اپنے تئیں تصوّر کرے اور دعا میں لگا رہے تب توحید کا نور خدا کی طرف سے اُس پر نازل ہوگا اور ایک نئی زندگی اُس کو بخشے گا۔

(حقیقۃ الوحی، روحانی خزائن جلد 22 صفحہ 148)

6- The Unity of God is a light which illumines the heart only after the negation of all deities, whether they belong to the inner world or the outer world. It permeates every particle of man's being. How can this be acquired without the aid of God and His Messenger? The duty of man is only to bring death upon his ego and turn his back to devilish pride. He should not boast of his having been reared in the cradle of knowledge but should consider himself as if he were merely an ignorant person, and occupy himself in supplications. Then the light of Unity will descend upon him from God and will bestow new life upon him.

(Haqiqatul Wahi: Roohani Khaza'in, Vol. 22, p. 148)

7۔ وہ خدا نہایت وفادار خدا ہے اور وفاداروں کے لئے اُس کے عجیب کام ظاہر ہوتے
ہیں دنیا چاہتی ہے کہ اُن کو کھا جائے اور ہر ایک دشمن اُن پر دانت پیتا ہے مگر وہ جو اُن
کا دوست ہے ہر ایک ہلاکت کی جگہ سے ان کو بچاتا ہے اور ہر ایک میدان میں اُن کو
فتح بخشتا ہے ۔ کیا ہی نیک طالع وہ شخص ہے جو اُس خدا کا دامن نہ چھوڑے ۔

(کشتی نوح ، روحانی خزائن جلد 19 صفحہ 20)

7- That God (presented by the Quran) is an extremely faithful
God, Who works wonders for those who remain faithful to
Him. The world is intent on destroying them (those faithful
to Him), but He Who befriends them delivers them from
every danger and bestows victory upon them in every field.
How singularly fortunate is he who never breaks ties with Him.

(Kashti Nuh: Roohani Khaza'in, Vol. 19, p. 20)

GOD'S TREATMENT OF PEOPLE LOYAL TO HIM

۸۔ درحقیقت وہ خدا بڑا زبردست اور قوی ہے جس کی طرف محبت اور وفا کے ساتھ جھکنے والے ہرگز ضائع نہیں کئے جاتے۔ دشمن کہتا ہے کہ مَیں اپنے منصوبوں سے ان کو ہلاک کردوں اور بداندیش ارادہ کرتا ہے کہ میں اُن کو کچل ڈالوں۔ مگر خدا کہتا ہے کہ اے نادان کیا تو میرے ساتھ لڑے گا؟ اور میرے عزیز کو ذلیل کر سکے گا؟ درحقیقت زمین پر کچھ نہیں ہوسکتا مگر وہی جو آسمان پر پہلے ہو چکا۔ اور کوئی زمین کا ہاتھ اس قدر سے زیادہ لمبا نہیں ہوسکتا جس قدر کہ وہ آسمان پر لمبا کیا گیا ہے۔ پس ظلم کے منصوبے باندھنے والے سخت نادان ہیں جو اپنے مکروہ اور قابل شرم منصوبوں کے وقت اس برتر ہستی کو یاد نہیں رکھتے جس کے ارادہ کے بغیر ایک پتّہ بھی نہیں گر سکتا۔ لہٰذا وہ اپنے ارادوں میں ہمیشہ ناکام اور شرمندہ رہتے ہیں اور ان کی بدی سے راستبازوں کو کوئی ضرر نہیں پہنچتا بلکہ خدا کے نشان ظاہر ہوتے ہیں اور خلق اللہ کی معرفت بڑھتی ہے۔ وہ قوی اور قادر خدا اگرچہ ان آنکھوں سے دکھائی نہیں دیتا مگر اپنے عجیب نشانوں سے اپنے تئیں ظاہر کر دیتا ہے۔

(کتاب البریہ مقدمہ، روحانی خزائن جلد 13 صفحہ 19۔20)

8-   Indeed, All Powerful and All Mighty is the God Whose devotees will not go to waste: those who come to Him with love and loyalty. The enemy boasts that he will annihilate them with his evil and ill- intentioned vows to stamp them out. Fools, says God, will you dare fight me and annihilate the one who is dear to Me? Indeed, nothing can happen on this earth unless it is so decreed in heaven, and no earthly hand can be stretched beyond the tether determined for it in heavens. Hence the plotters of evil and cruel designs are most foolish who, during their abhorrent and shameless conspiracies, do not remember that Supreme Being without Whose express decree not a leaf is permitted to fall. Therefore, they remain unsuccessful and frustrated in their objectives: and the rightly guided are not harmed by their evil. Instead, the signs of God are widely manifested and people's understanding of God's ways is enhanced. That All Powerful and Mighty God Who remains unseen by the eyes manifests Himself indeed through His wondrous ways.

(Kitabul Bariyya, Muqaddama: Roohani Khaza'in, Vol. 13, pp. 19-20)

9۔ خدا آسمان و زمین کا نور ہے۔ یعنے ہر ایک نور جو بلندی اور پستی میں نظر آتا ہے خواہ وہ ارواح میں ہے خواہ اجسام میں، اور خواہ ذاتی ہے اور خواہ عرضی، اور خواہ ظاہری ہے اور خواہ باطنی، اور خواہ ذہنی ہے خواہ خارجی اُسی کے فیض کا عطیہ ہے۔ یہ اِس بات کی طرف اشارہ ہے کہ حضرت ربّ العالمین کا فیضِ عام ہر چیز پر محیط ہو رہا ہے اور کوئی اس کے فیض سے خالی نہیں۔ وہی تمام فیوض کا مبدء ہے اور تمام انوار کا علّت العلل اور تمام رحمتوں کا سرچشمہ ہے۔ اُسی کی ہستی حقیقی تمام عالَم کی قیوم اور تمام زیر و زبر کی پناہ ہے۔ وہی ہے جس نے ہر ایک چیز کو ظلمت خانہ عدم سے باہر نکالا اور خلعتِ وجود بخشا۔ بجز اس کے کوئی ایسا وجود نہیں ہے کہ جو فی حدّ ذاتہٖ واجب اور قدیم ہو۔ یا اِس سے مستفیض نہ ہو بلکہ خاک اور افلاک اور انسان اور حیوان اور حجر اور شجر اور روح اور جسم سب اُسی کے فیضان سے وجود پذیر ہیں۔

(براہین احمدیہ حاشیہ، روحانی خزائن جلد 1 صفحہ 191-192)

9- God is the light of the heavens and the earth. Every light that is seen, be it high or low, whether it belongs to souls or pertains to bodies, or be it substantive or attributive, whether hidden or evident, be it subjective or objective, it is a mere bounty of His Grace. This is a sign which indicates that the bounties of Allah encompass everything. He is the source of all Grace and is the ultimate cause of every light, the Fountainhead of all mercies. His Being is the support of the universe and is the refuge of all, high and low. He it is Who brought everything out of the darkness of nothingness and bestowed upon everything the mantle of being. No being other than He exists by itself or is eternal. All other beings are recipients of His grace. Earth and heaven, man and beast, stones and trees, souls and bodies, all are sustained by His Grace.

(Braheen Ahmadiyya, footnote: Roohani Khaza'in, Vol. 1, pp.191-192)

10۔ حمد و ثنا اُسی کو جو ذات جاودانی

ہمسر نہیں ہے اُس کا کوئی نہ کوئی ثانی

باقی وہی ہمیشہ غیر اُس کے سب ہیں فانی

غیروں سے دل لگانا جھوٹی ہے سب کہانی

سب غیر ہیں وہی ہے اِک دل کا یار جانی

دل میں میرے یہی ہے سُبْحَانَ مَنْ یَّرَانِیْ

سب کا وہی سہارا رحمت ہے آشکارا

ہم کو وہی پیارا دلبر وہی ہمارا

اُس بن نہیں گزارا غیر اُس کے جھوٹ سارا

یہ روز کر مبارک سُبْحَانَ مَنْ یَّرَانِیْ

(محمود کی آمین، روحانی خزائن جلد 12 صفحہ 319)

10- All praise be unto Him Who is the Everlasting,
     None is His equal, nor is anything like unto Him.
     He remains forever, the rest is transient,
     To love others than Him is a mere fantasy.
     He alone is my heart's desire, I know none other,
     My heart exclaims: Holy is He Who keeps me in sight.
     He provides for all, His Grace is manifest,
     In Him alone lies our comfort; He alone is dear to us.
     Without Him we cannot live, all else is false,
     Blessed be this day, Holy is He Who keeps me in sight.
                    (Mahmood Ki Ameen: Roohani Khaza'in, Vol. 12, p. 319)

THE HOLY PROPHET

(peace and blessings of Allah be upon him)

۱۱۔ وہ اعلیٰ درجہ کا نور جو انسان کو دیا گیا یعنی انسانِ کامل کو وہ ملائک میں نہیں تھا، نجوم میں نہیں تھا، قمر میں نہیں تھا، آفتاب میں بھی نہیں تھا۔ وہ زمین کے سمندروں اور دریاؤں میں بھی نہیں تھا۔ وہ لعل اور یاقوت اور زمرد اور الماس اور موتی میں بھی نہیں تھا۔ غرض وہ کسی چیز ارضی اور سماوی میں نہیں تھا۔ صرف انسان میں تھا یعنی انسانِ کامل میں جس کا اتم اور اکمل اور اعلیٰ اور ارفع فرد ہمارے سیّد و مولیٰ سیّد الانبیاء سیّد الاحیاء محمد مصطفیٰ صلی اللہ علیہ وسلم ہیں۔ سو وہ نُور رأس انسان کو دیا گیا اور حسب مراتب اُس کے تمام ہم رنگوں کو بھی یعنی اُن لوگوں کو بھی جو کسی قدر روہی رنگ رکھتے ہیں .... اور یہ شان اعلیٰ اور اکمل اور اتم طور پر ہمارے سید، ہمارے مولیٰ، ہمارے ہادی، نبی امی، صادق مصدوق محمد مصطفیٰ صلی اللہ علیہ وسلم میں پائی جاتی تھی۔

(آئینہ کمالاتِ اسلام، روحانی خزائن جلد ۵ صفحہ ۱۶۰-۱۶۲)

11-The sublime light which was bestowed on man, i.e., the most perfect among them, was not shared by angels nor by stars; nor was it in the moon, nor in the sun, or in the oceans and the rivers. It was not to be found in rubies or emeralds, nor in sapphires, nor in pearls: It was not in any earthly or heavenly object. It was possessed only by the perfect man, manifested in the most consummate way in the person of our lord and master, Muhammad, the chosen one, the chief of all the prophets, leader of those who live (in the sight of Allah). So, that light was bestowed on that man and likewise, to a degree, on all who in their several ways were similar to him... Sublime grace was possessed in its most perfect and consummate manifestation by our lord and master, the unlettered Prophet, the truthful one, the one whose truth is testified to, Muhammad, the chosen one, peace be on him.

(Ayena Kamalat e Islam: Roohani Khaza'in, Vol. 5, pp. 160-162).

۔12 مَیں ہمیشہ تعجب کی نگہ سے دیکھتا ہوں کہ یہ عربی نبی جس کا نام محمد ہے (ہزار ہزار درود اور سلام اُس پر) یہ کس عالی مرتبہ کا نبی ہے۔ اُس کے عالی مقام کا انتہا معلوم نہیں ہو سکتا اور اُس کی تاثیر قدسی کا اندازہ کرنا انسان کا کام نہیں۔ افسوس کہ جیسا حق شناخت کا ہے اُس کے مرتبہ کو شناخت نہیں کیا گیا۔ وہ توحید جو دنیا سے گم ہو چکی تھی وہی ایک پہلوان ہے جو دوبارہ اُس کو دنیا میں لایا۔ اُس نے خدا سے انتہائی درجہ پر محبت کی اور انتہائی درجہ پر بنی نوع کی ہمدردی میں اس کی جان گداز ہوئی اِس لئے خدا نے جو اُس کے دل کے راز کا واقف تھا اُس کو تمام انبیاء اور تمام اوّلین و آخرین پر فضیلت بخشی اور اُس کی مرادیں اُس کی زندگی میں اُس کو دیں۔

(حقیقۃ الوحی، روحانی خزائن جلد 22 صفحہ 118ـ119)

12-I look always with wonder at this Arab Prophet whose name is Muhammad, thousands of blessings and peace be upon him. How exalted his status was! One cannot perceive the ultimate limit of his station, and it is not within the scope of man to fully comprehend the depth and penetration of his ennobling qualities. Alas! Due recognition has not been paid to his lofty rank. That unity which had disappeared from the world was restored by this same valiant champion. He loved God most intensely, so also his soul was consumed in deep sympathy for mankind. That is why God, Who was fully aware of the hidden excellences of his heart, exalted him above all the Prophets and all the people of the past and the future, and fulfilled his heart's desires in the span of his lifetime.

(Haqiqatul Wahi: Roohani Khaza'in, Vol.22, pp. 118-119)

13۔ ہمارے نبی صلی اللہ علیہ وسلم تمام انبیاء کے نام اپنے اندر جمع رکھتے ہیں کیونکہ وہ وجود پاک جامع کمالاتِ متفرقہ ہے۔ پس وہ موسیٰ بھی ہے اور عیسیٰ بھی اور آدم بھی اور ابراہیم بھی اور یوسف بھی اور یعقوب بھی۔ اسی کی طرف اللہ جلّ شانہٗ اشارہ فرماتا ہے۔ فَبِهُدَاهُمُ اقْتَدِهْ (سورۃ الانعام:91) یعنی اے رسول اللہ! تُو اُن تمام ہدایات متفرقہ کو اپنے وجود میں جمع کر لے جو ہر ایک نبی خاص طور پر اپنے ساتھ رکھتا تھا۔ پس اس سے ثابت ہے کہ تمام انبیاء کی شانیں آنحضرت صلی اللہ علیہ وسلم کی ذات میں شامل تھیں اور درحقیقت محمدؐ کا نام صلی اللہ علیہ وسلم اسی کی طرف اشارہ کرتا ہے۔ کیونکہ محمدؐ کے یہ معنے ہیں کہ بغایت تعریف کیا گیا اور غایت درجہ کی تعریف تبھی متصوّر ہو سکتی ہے کہ جب انبیاء کے تمام کمالاتِ متفرقہ اور صفات خاصّہ آنحضرت صلی اللہ علیہ وسلم میں جمع ہوں۔

(آئینہ کمالاتِ اسلام، روحانی خزائن جلد 5 صفحہ 343)

13-Our Holy Prophet, peace and blessings of Allah be on him, combines in him the names of all the prophets, for in him are blended the noble qualities we find only singly in all the other prophets. Hence, he is Moses as well as Jesus; he is Adam, he is Abraham, he is Joseph and also he is Jacob. God indicates that in the verse: فبهداهم اقتده "So do thou follow their guidance." (6:91):Meaning: 0 Prophet of God, merge in yourself the various teachings of all the prophets! This shows that the excellence of all the prophets was combined in the Holy Prophet, peace and blessings of Allah be upon him. In fact the very name Muhammad points towards this because it means "the one who is most highly praised." The highest praise can only be conceived if it is granted that the very best virtues and special qualities of all the prophets are blended in him.

(Ayena Kamalat e Islam: Roohani Khaza'in, Vol. 5, p. 343)

۱۴۔ مجھے سمجھایا گیا ہے کہ تمام رسولوں میں سے کامل تعلیم دینے والا اور اعلیٰ درجہ کی پاک اور پُر حکمت تعلیم دینے والا اور انسانی کمالات کا اپنی زندگی کے ذریعہ سے اعلیٰ نمونہ دکھلانے والا صرف حضرت سیدنا و مولانا محمد مصطفیٰ صلی اللہ علیہ وسلم ہیں۔

(اربعین 1، روحانی خزائن جلد 17 صفحہ 345)

14-I have been made to understand that of all the Messengers, the one who gave the most perfect and purest of teachings full of wisdom, and the one who exhibited in him the noblest of human qualities, is the Holy Prophet Muhammad, our lord and master, may peace and blessings of Allah be upon him.   *(Arbaeen, No. 1: Roohani Khaza'in, Vol. 17, p. 345)*

۱۵۔ ہم جب انصاف کی نظر سے دیکھتے ہیں تو تمام سلسلۂ نبوت میں سے اعلیٰ درجہ کا جوانمرد نبیؐ اور زندہ نبیؐ اور خدا کا اعلیٰ درجہ کا پیارا نبیؐ صرف ایک مرد کو جانتے ہیں یعنی وہی نبیوں کا سردار، رسولوں کا فخر، تمام مُرسَلوں کا سرتاج جس کا نام محمد مصطفیٰ و احمد مجتبیٰ صلی اللہ علیہ وسلم ہے۔   (سراجِ منیر، روحانی خزائن جلد 12 صفحہ 82)

15-When we examine with fairness and justice all the prophets of the past, we find that Muhammad, the Holy Prophet of Islam, stands out as the most valiant among them, the one who fully possessed all the qualities of life and was the one most endeared to God.

(Siraj-e-Muneer: Roohani Khaza'in, Vol. 12, p. 82)

۱۶۔ وہ جو عرب کے بیابانی ملک میں ایک عجیب ماجرا گزرا کہ لاکھوں مُردے تھوڑے
دنوں میں زندہ ہو گئے اور پُشتوں کے بگڑے ہوئے اِلٰہی رنگ پکڑ گئے۔اور آنکھوں
کے اندھے بینا ہوئے۔اور گونگوں کی زبان پر اِلٰہی معارف جاری ہوئے۔اور دُنیا
میں یکدفعہ ایک ایسا انقلاب پیدا ہوا کہ نہ پہلے اِس سے کسی آنکھ نے دیکھا اور نہ کسی
کان نے سُنا۔کچھ جانتے ہو کہ وہ کیا تھا؟ وہ ایک فانی فی اللہ کی اندھیری راتوں کی
دُعائیں ہی تھیں جنہوں نے دُنیا میں شور مچا دیا۔اور وہ عجائب باتیں دکھلائیں کہ جو
اُس اُمّی بیکس سے محالات کی طرح نظر آتی تھیں۔اَللّٰھُمَّ صَلِّ وَ سَلِّمْ وَ بَارِکْ
عَلَیْہِ وَ اٰلِہٖ بِعَدَدِ ھَمِّہٖ وَ غَمِّہٖ وَ حُزْنِہٖ لِھٰذِہِ الْاُمَّۃِ وَ اَنْزِلْ عَلَیْہِ اَنْوَارَ رَحْمَتِکَ
اِلَی الْاَبَدِ۔ (برکات الدعا، روحانی خزائن جلد 6 صفحہ 11-10)

16-A strange phenomenal event took place in the deserts of
Arabia, when hundreds of thousands of dead became alive
within a few days, and those who had been corrupted
through generations took on Divine colour. The blind began
to see and the tongues of the dumb began to flow with
Divine wisdom. Such a revolution took place in the world
as no eye had seen or no ear had heard of before. Do you
realize what this was? All this was brought about by prayers
during the darkness of night of one who had been wholly
lost in God. This created an uproar in the world and
manifested such wonders as seemed impossible at the hands
of that unlettered helpless person. 0 Allah! Send down
blessings and peace on him and on his followers in
proportion to his concern and suffering for the Muslim Ummah
(the people of Islam), and shower upon him the light of Thy
mercy forever.

(Barakatud Dua: Roohani Khaza'in, Vol. 6, pp. 10-11)

17 ۔تمام آدم زادوں کیلئے اب کوئی رسول اور شفیع نہیں مگر محمد مصطفیٰ صلی اللہ علیہ وسلم ۔سوم کوشش کرو کہ سچی محبت اس جاہ و جلال کے نبی کے ساتھ رکھو اور اُس کے غیر کو اُس پر کسی نوع کی بڑائی مت دو تا آسمان پر تم نجات یافتہ لکھے جاؤ۔ اور یاد رکھو کہ نجات وہ چیز نہیں جو مرنے کے بعد ظاہر ہوگی بلکہ حقیقی نجات وہ ہے کہ اسی دنیا میں اپنی روشنی دکھلاتی ہے ۔ نجات یافتہ کون ہے؟ وہ جو یقین رکھتا ہے جو خدا سچ ہے اور محمد صلی اللہ علیہ وسلم اس میں اور تمام مخلوق میں درمیانی شفیع ہے اور آسمان کے نیچے نہ اس کے ہم مرتبہ کوئی اور رسول ہے اور نہ قرآن کے ہم رتبہ کوئی اور کتاب ہے۔ اور کسی کے لئے خدا نے نہ چاہا کہ وہ ہمیشہ زندہ رہے مگر یہ برگزیدہ نبی ہمیشہ کے لئے زندہ ہے۔

(کشتی نوح، روحانی خزائن جلد 19 صفحہ 14-13)

17-For all the children of Adam there is now no Messenger and intercessor other than the Holy Prophet Muhammad, the chosen one, may peace and blessings of Allah be upon him. So you should endeavor to cultivate true love for this magnificent and majestic prophet and not place anyone else above him in any manner so that you may be counted in Heaven among those who have attained salvation. Remember, salvation is not something which is attainable only after death. Indeed true salvation is the one which manifests its light in this very world. Who is the one who is delivered? He indeed who believes that God is truth and that the Holy Prophet, may peace and blessings of Allah be upon him, is the intercessor between God and mankind. So also he believes that under the firmament of Heaven there is no prophet equal to him and that there is no book of the status of the Quran. And for none else God ordained that he should live forever with his message and his law, but this noble Prophet lives forever.

(Kashti Nuh: Roohani Khaza'in Vol. 19, p.13-14)

18۔واقعات حضرت خاتم الانبیاء صلی اللہ علیہ وسلم پر نظر کرنے سے یہ بات نہایت واضح اور نمایاں اور روشن ہے کہ آنحضرت اعلیٰ درجہ کے یک رنگ اور صاف باطن اور خدا کے لئے جان باز اور خلقت کے بیم و امید سے بالکل منہ پھیرنے والے اور محض خدا پر توکل کرنے والے تھے کہ جنہوں نے خدا کی خواہش اور مرضی میں محو اور فنا ہو کر اس بات کی کچھ بھی پروانہ کی کہ توحید کی مُنادی کرنے سے کیا کیا بلا میرے سر پر آوے گی اور مشرکوں کے ہاتھ سے کیا کچھ دکھ اور درد اٹھانا ہوگا۔

(براہین احمدیہ، روحانی خزائن جلد 1 صفحہ 111)

18-From a study of the life of the Holy Prophet, peace and blessings of Allah be upon him, it will become manifest to every reader that the Holy Prophet of Islam had no duality in his character and possessed a pure and noble spirit. He was ever ready to lay down his life for God. He pinned no hopes on men and he entertained no fear of them. He reposed his entire trust in Allah. Having enslaved himself entirely to the will and pleasure of Allah, he cared not what hazards he would face and what suffering he would be subjected to at the hands of the idolaters as a result of declaring to the world the message of the Unity of God.

(Braheen Ahmadiyya: Roohani Khaza'in, Vol. 1, p. 111)

19۔کیا یہ حیرت انگیز ماجرا نہیں ہے کہ ایک بے زر، بے زور، بیکس، اُمّی، یتیم، تنہا، غریب ایسے زمانہ میں کہ جس میں ہر ایک قوم پوری پوری طاقت مالی اور فوجی اور علمی رکھتی تھی ایسی روشن تعلیم لایا کہ اپنی براہین قاطعہ اور حجج واضحہ سے سب کی زبان بند کر دی اور بڑے بڑے لوگوں کی جو حکیم بنے پھرتے تھے اور فیلسوف کہلاتے تھے فاش غلطیاں نکالیں اور پھر باوجود بے کسی اور غربی کے زور سے ایسا بھی دکھایا کہ بادشاہوں کو تختوں سے گرا دیا اور اُنہیں تختوں پر غریبوں کو بٹھایا۔ اگر یہ خدا کی تائید نہیں تھی تو اور کیا تھی۔

کیا تمام دنیا پر عقل اور علم اور طاقت اور زور میں غالب آ جانا بغیر تائید الٰہی کے بھی ہوا کرتا ہے؟ (براہین احمدیہ، روحانی خزائن جلد 1 صفحہ 119)

19-Is it not a most wonderful thing to have happened that in an age when all the great nations of the world possessed a plenitude of financial, military and intellectual means, a mere penniless orphan, who was powerless, helpless, unlettered and unaided, brought forth such resplendent teachings which, with their conclusive arguments and irrefutable proofs, dumb-founded every opponent? It also exposed the mistakes and faults of such scholars who in their conceit boasted of being great philosophers and men of wisdom. In spite of his being poor and helpless, he rose to great power and dethroned many a mighty king and in their place installed the poor. If this was not from Allah, what else was it? To conquer and excel the whole world in wisdom, in knowledge and in strength, can all this be accomplished without the help of Allah?

(Braheen Ahmadiyya: Roohani Khaza'in, Vol.1, p. 191)

20۔ اسی طرح حضرت داؤد علیہ السلام نے آنحضرت صلی اللہ علیہ وسلم کی جلالیت و عظمت کا اقرار کر کے زبور پینتالیس میں یوں بیان کیا ہے (2) تو حسن میں بنی آدم سے کہیں زیادہ ہے۔ تیرے لبوں میں نعمت بتائی گئی ہے اسی لئے خدا نے تجھ کو ابد تک مبارک کیا (3) اے پہلوان تو جاہ و جلال سے اپنی تلوار حمائل کر کے اپنی ران پر لٹکا (4) امانت اور حلم اور عدالت پر اپنی بزرگواری اور اقبال مندی سے سوار ہو کہ تیرا داہنا ہاتھ تجھے ہیبت ناک کام دکھائے گا۔ (سرمہ چشم آریہ، روحانی خزائن جلد 2 صفحہ 281۔282 حاشیہ)

20-David, on whom be peace, affirmed the greatness and grandeur of the Holy Prophet, may peace and blessings of

Allah be on him, when he said in Psalm 45:

(2) You indeed are far more handsome than the sons of men.

Charm has been poured out upon your lips.

That is why God has blessed you till eternity.

(3) Gird your sword (upon) your thigh, 0 mighty one,

(With) your dignity and your splendour.

(4) And in your splendour go proceed to victory.

Ride in the cause of truth with humility and righteousness,

And your right hand will instruct you in fear inspiring things.

(Surma Chashm Arya: Roohani Khaza'in, Vol. 2, p. 281 282)

۲۱۔خیال کرنا چاہئے کہ کس استقلال سے آنحضرتؐ اپنے دعویٰ نبوت پر باوجود پیدا
ہوجانے ہزاروں خطرات اور کھڑے ہوجانے لاکھوں معاندوں اور مزاحموں اور
ڈرانے والوں کے اوّل سے اخیر دم تک ثابت اور قائم رہے۔ برسوں تک وہ مصیبتیں
دیکھیں اور وہ دکھ اٹھانے پڑے جو کامیابی سے بکّلی مایوس کرتے تھے اور روز بروز
بڑھتے جاتے تھے کہ جن پر صبر کرنے سے کسی دنیوی مقصد کا حاصل ہوجانا وہم بھی
نہیں گزرتا تھا بلکہ نبوت کا دعویٰ کرنے سے از دست اپنی پہلی جمعیت کو بھی کھو بیٹھے
اور ایک بات کہہ کر لاکھ تفرقہ خرید لیا اور ہزاروں بلاؤں کو اپنے سر پر بلا لیا۔ وطن سے
نکالے گئے۔ قتل کے لئے تعاقب کئے گئے۔ گھر اور اسباب تباہ اور برباد ہو گیا۔ بارہا
زہر دی گئی۔ اور جو خیر خواہ تھے وہ بدخواہ بن گئے۔ اور جو دوست تھے وہ دشمنی کرنے
لگے۔ اور ایک زمانہ دراز تک وہ تلخیاں اٹھانی پڑیں کہ جن پر ثابت قدمی سے ٹھہرے
رہنا کسی فریبی اور مکّار کا کام نہیں۔   (براہین احمدیہ، روحانی خزائن جلد ۱ صفحہ ۱۰۸-۱۰۹)

21-Take note how the Holy Prophet of Islam remained resolute
and steadfast in his claim to prophethood from beginning to

end in the face of thousands of dangers and a multitude of enemies and threatening opponents. For years on end he endured such hardships and sufferings as increased from day to day; enough to make one despair of success. It is inconceivable for a man with ulterior worldly motives to have shown such prolonged and steadfast endurance. Not only that, by putting forth his claim to prophethood, he even lost the support he previously enjoyed. The price he had to pay for his one claim was to confront a hundred thousand contentions and invite a multitude of calamities to befall upon his head. He was exiled from his homeland; pursued with intent to murder; his home and belongings were destroyed. Several attempts were made on his life by poisoning. Those who were his well wishers began to harbour ill for him. Friends turned into foes. For an age which seemed an eternity he braved such hardships as are beyond a pretender and impostor to suffer through.

(Braheen Ahmadiyya: Roohani Khaza'in, Vol. 1, pp. 108-109)

22۔ اور میرے لئے اس نعمت کا پانا ممکن نہ تھا اگر مَیں اپنے سیّد و مولٰی فخر الانبیاء اور خیر الورٰی حضرت محمد مصطفیٰ صلی اللہ علیہ وسلم کے راہوں کی پیروی نہ کرتا۔ سو مَیں نے جو کچھ پایا اُس پَیروی سے پایا۔ اور مَیں اپنے سچے اور کامل علم سے جانتا ہوں کہ کوئی انسان بجز پَیروی اُس نبی صلی اللہ علیہ وسلم کے خدا تک نہیں پہنچ سکتا اور نہ معرفت کاملہ کا حصّہ پا سکتا ہے۔ اور مَیں اِس جگہ یہ بھی بتلاتا ہوں کہ وہ کیا چیز ہے کہ سچی اور کامل پَیروی آنحضرت صلی اللہ علیہ وسلم کے بعد سب باتوں سے پہلے دل میں پیدا ہوتی ہے۔ سو یاد رہے کہ وہ قلبِ سلیم ہے یعنی دل سے دنیا کی محبت نکل جاتی ہے اور دل ایک ابدی اور لازوال لذّت کا طالب ہو جاتا ہے۔ پھر بعد اس کے ایک مصفّٰی اور کامل

22-It would not have been possible for me to have attained this grace if I had not followed the footsteps of my lord and master, the pride of all the prophets, the best of mankind, Muhammad, the chosen one, peace and blessings of Allah be upon him. Whatever I have achieved, I have achieved by following him, and I know from verified reliable experience that no man can reach God and obtain a deeper understanding of His ways without following that Prophet, may peace and blessings of Allah be upon him. Now, let me also make it known that the very first thing you are rewarded with, after having completely submitted yourself to the instructions and teachings of the Holy Prophet Muhammad, is that you are granted a new heart which is always rightly inclined, that is to say, a heart which has turned cold upon the love of this material world, and instead it begins to yearn for an everlasting heavenly pleasure. Having achieved this desire this heart is now fit to receive tha t perfect and purest love, the love of God. Because of your complete obedience to him, all these blessings are bequeathed to you as his spiritual heritage.

(Haqeeqatul Wahi: Roohani Khaza'in, Vol. 22, pp. 64-65)

23۔ مصطفٰیؐ پر ترا بے حد ہو سلام اور رحمت

اس سے یہ نور لیا بارِ خدایا ہم نے

ربط ہے جان محمدؐ سے مری جاں کو مدام

دل کو وہ جام لبالب ہے پلایا ہم نے

اُس سے بہتر نظر آیا نہ کوئی عالم میں

لاجرم غیروں سے دل اپنا چھڑایا ہم نے

شانِ حق تیرے شمائل میں نظر آتی ہے

تیرے پانے سے ہی اُس ذات کو پایا ہم نے

چُھو کے دامن ترا ہر دام سے ملتی ہے نجات

لاجرم دَر پہ ترے سر کو جھکایا ہم نے

دلبرا مجھ کو قسم ہے تری یکتائی کی

آپ کو تیری محبت میں بھلایا ہم نے

بخدا دل سے مرے مٹ گئے سب غیروں کے نقش

جب سے دل میں یہ ترا نقش جمایا ہم نے

ہم ہوئے خیرِ اُمم تجھ سے ہی اے خیرِ رُسل

تیرے بڑھنے سے قدم آگے بڑھایا ہم نے

آدمی زاد تو کیا چیز فرشتے بھی تمام

مدح میں تیری وہ گاتے ہیں جو گایا ہم نے

(آئینہ کمالاتِ اسلام، روحانی خزائن جلد 5 صفحہ 225-226)

23-Thy boundless blessings and peace
   be upon Mustafa, 0 God;
   Verily through him we receive Thy light.

   My soul is eternally bonded
   to the soul of Muhammad.
   I made my heart drink deep,
   of the brimful cup of this love.

None better than he could
I discover in the whole world.
Most certainly,
I have broken my heart loose
from the grip of others.

God's glory is reflected
in your virtues my beloved.
Him I made my own,
by having made you mine.

Having touched the hem
of Thy garment, 0 God,
One is saved from being entrapped,
by the charms of others.
Verily, I bow my head
at your threshold alone.

O my beloved,
I swear by Thy Unity,
In my love of Thee I have become
oblivious to my own self.

By God, all other images
have vanished from my heart.
Ever since I had,
Your countenance etched upon it.

It was because of you that we
became the best of all the peoples,
O Prophet of God who
is the best of all the prophets.
As you marched ahead of all the rest,
we too stepped forward.

Let alone the human beings,
even all the angels in the Heavens
follow suit and join me,
as I sing Thy praise.

(Ayena e Kamalate Islam: Roohani Khaza'in Vol 5, pp 225 -226)

24۔ وہ پیشوا ہمارا ، جس سے ہے نور سارا

نام اُس کا ہے محمدؐ ، دلبر مرا یہی ہے

سب پاک ہیں پیمبر ، اک دوسرے سے بہتر

لیک از خدائے برتر خیرالوریٰ یہی ہے

پہلوں سے خوب تر ہے ، خوبی میں اک قمر ہے

اُس پر ہر اک نظر ہے ، بدرالدجیٰ یہی ہے

پہلے تو رہ میں ہارے ، پار اُس نے ہیں اتارے

میں جاؤں اُس کے وارے بس ناخدا یہی ہے

وہ یار لامکانی ، وہ دلبر نہانی

دیکھا ہے ہم نے اُس سے بس رہنما یہی ہے

وہ آج شاہِ دیں ہے ، وہ تاجِ مرسلیں ہے

وہ طیب و امیں ہے ، اس کی ثنا یہی ہے

آنکھ اُس کی دوربیں ہے ، دل یار سے قریں ہے

ہاتھوں میں شمع دیں ہے ، عین الضیا یہی ہے

جو رازِ دیں تھے بھارے ، اس نے بتائے سارے

دولت کا دینے والا فرماں روا یہی ہے

اُس نور پر فدا ہوں اُس کا ہی میں ہوا ہوں

وہ ہے میں چیز کیا ہوں ، بس فیصلہ یہی ہے

(قادیان کے آریہ اور ہم ، روحانی خزائن جلد 20 صفحہ 456)

24-That leader of ours,
    from whom radiates all light,
    his name is Muhammad.
    He is the one
    who has captivated my heart.

    All prophets are holy,
    One better than the other.
    But from God on high,
    he is the crown of all creatures.

    Superior to all
    the earlier ones,
    he shines forth
    like a moon in excellence.

    Each gaze is fixed upon him,
    He indeed is the full moon,
    Which lights up the darkness.

    Those before him
    gave up half way through.
    He is the one,
    who steered safely,
    to the destined heaven.
    May that I lay down,
    my life in his cause.
    He alone is the perfect master.

That Beloved unbounded by space,
that Darling of the recesses of my heart.
Was shown to us by him (Muhammad),
unique is he in guidance.

Today he is the sovereign,
of the world of religion,
the crown of all the Messengers.
The healthiest influence;
The purest, the most comely;
The most trustworthy;
The most dependable:
Allah! This superlative praise;
befits him alone.

His eye
Ranges far and wide,
Like a powerful telescope;
While his heart remains
Incessantly close
To the Lord God!
In his hand he carries
The Torch of religion;
And this alone is the real
And true source of light!

Whatsoever the great secrets
In the domain of religion,
He has opened all knots,
No matter how subtle,
And how strong;
And he alone is the king,
In a position to distribute
This – the rarest

Of all kinds of wealth!

Indeed I am sold,
Entirely, On this light:
Wholly, and completely,
Am I devoted to it;
In my mind, in this respect,
There are no reservations!
He alone is the one
That counts; while I,
In myself, amount
Absolutely, to nothing:
This alone is the basic
Truth; This alone
The final verdict.

(Qadian Ke Arya Aur Hum: Roohani Khaza'in, Vol. 20, p. 456)

THE HOLY QURAN

۲۵۔قرآن جواہرات کی تھیلی ہے اورلوگ اس سے بے خبر ہیں!

(ملفوظات جلد 2 صفحہ 542۔ ایڈیشن 2003ء)

25-The Holy Quran is a treasure chest, but few are those who are aware of it. *(Malfoozat Vol. 2: p 344)*

۲۶۔قرآن کی وہ اعلیٰ شان ہے کہ ہر ایک شان سے بلند ہے۔ وہ حَکم ہے یعنی فیصلہ کرنے والا اور وہ مہیمن ہے یعنی تمام ہدایتوں کا مجموعہ ہے۔ اس نے تمام دلیلیں جمع کردیں اور دشمنوں کی جمعیت کو تتّر بتّر کردیا۔ اور وہ ایسی کتاب ہے کہ اُس میں ہر چیز کی تفصیل ہے۔ اور اُس میں آئندہ اور گزشتہ کی خبریں موجود ہیں۔ اور باطل کو اس کی طرف راہ نہیں ہے نہ آگے سے نہ پیچھے سے۔ اور وہ خدا تعالیٰ کا نور ہے۔

(خطبہ الہامیہ، روحانی خزائن جلد 16 صفحہ 103)

26-The Holy Quran is so glorious that none other can excel it in its glory. It is Hakam, the one whose judgment is ultimate; it is Muhaimin, a compendium of all guidance. Therein is found every argument which one may require. It is this Book which has scattered in defeat the very core of the enemy's might. A Book which covers everything in depth and contains the news of what was and what is to be. Falsehood can attack it not from the front nor from the rear. It is the very light of God Almighty.

(Khutba Ilhamiya: Roohani Khaza'in Vol. 16, p. 103)

۲۷۔ جاننا چاہئے کہ کھلا کھلا اعجاز قرآن شریف کا جو ہر ایک قوم اور ہر ایک اہل زبان پر روشن ہوسکتا ہے جس کو پیش کرکے ہم ہر ایک ملک کے آدمی کو خواہ وہ ہندی ہو یا پارسی یا یورپین یا امریکن یا کسی اور ملک کا ہو ملزم و ساکت و لاجواب کرسکتے ہیں۔ وہ غیر محدود معارف و حقائق و علوم حکمیہ قرآنیہ ہیں جو ہر زمانہ میں اُس زمانہ کی حاجت کے موافق کھلتے جاتے ہیں اور ہر ایک زمانہ کے خیالات کا مقابلہ کرنے کے لئے مسلح سپاہیوں کی طرح کھڑے ہیں۔ اگر قرآن شریف اپنے حقائق و دقائق کے لحاظ سے ایک محدود چیز ہوتی تو ہرگز وہ معجزہ تامّہ نہیں ٹھہر سکتا تھا۔

(ازالہ اوہام حصہ اوّل، روحانی خزائن جلد ۳ صفحہ ۲۵۵۔۲۵۶)

27-Let it be known that the most outstanding miracle of the Holy Quran is that boundless sea of deep wisdom those solid facts, those avenues of Quranic knowledge so rich in philosophy which we can manifestly present to all nations and peoples of every language: be they Indians, Persians, Europeans or Americans, whichever country they belong to. The Quranic miracle is capable of rendering them defenceless, speechless and totally disarmed. The meanings of the Holy Quran are unfolded as demand is created according to the changing times and stand guard like well armed soldiers against the insinuations and aspersions cast in every age. Had the Quran been limited in extent regarding that which it comprises of solid facts and subtle realities it could not have been deemed as that perfect miracle.

(Izala e Auham, Pt. 1: Roohani Khaza'in Vol. 3, pg. 255)

۲۸۔ قرآن شریف ایسا معجزہ ہے کہ نہ وہ اول مثل ہوا اور نہ آخر کبھی ہوگا۔ اس کے فیوض و برکات کا در ہمیشہ جاری ہے اور وہ ہر زمانہ میں اسی طرح نمایاں اور درخشاں ہے جیسا آنحضرت صلی اللہ علیہ وسلم کے وقت تھا۔ علاوہ اس کے یہ بھی یاد رکھنا چاہئے کہ

ہر شخص کا کلام اس کی ہمت کے موافق ہوتا ہے ۔ جس قدر اس کی ہمت اور عزم اور مقاصد عالی ہوں گے اسی پایہ کا وہ کلام ہوگا ۔ اور وحی الٰہی میں بھی یہی رنگ ہوتا ہے ۔ جس شخص کی طرف اس کی وحی آتی ہے جس قدر ہمت بلند رکھنے والا وہ ہوگا اسی پایہ کا کلام اسے ملے گا ۔ آنحضرت صلی اللہ علیہ وسلم کی ہمت واستعداد اور عزم کا دائرہ چونکہ بہت ہی وسیع تھا اس لئے آپ کو جو کلام ملا وہ بھی اس پایہ اور رُتبہ کا ہے کہ دوسرا کوئی شخص اس ہمت اور حوصلہ کا کبھی پیدا نہ ہوگا ‘‘ ۔ (ملفوظات جلد دوم صفحہ 40-41)

28- The Holy Quran is a miracle the like of which never was and never will be. The age of its blessings and bounties is everlasting. It remains as manifest and radiant in any other period as it was in the period of the Holy Prophet of Islam, peace be upon him. It should also be kept in mind that the speech of man is directly proportional to the vastness of his resolve, aptitude and determination. The greater his aptitude and determination and motivation, the more exquisite will be the quality of his speech. The same is the case of revelations from God. The loftier the aptitude of the recipient of revelation, the more sublime will be the quality of the word of God. In proportion to the vastness of his resolve, aptitude and determination, the revelation bestowed upon him was of the highest order, hence none can ever be born to equal him in this regard.

(Malfoozat Vol. 2, p. 40-41, edition 2003)

29۔ ہم سچ سچ کہتے ہیں اور سچ کہنے سے کسی حالت میں رک نہیں سکتے کہ اگر آنحضرت صلی اللہ علیہ وسلم آ ئے نہ ہوتے اور قرآن شریف جس کی تاثیریں ہمارے ائمّہ اور اکابر قدیم سے دیکھتے آ ئے اور آج ہم دیکھ رہے ہیں، نازل نہ ہوا ہوتا تو ہمارے لئے یہ امر بڑا ہی مشکل ہوتا کہ جو ہم فقط بائبل کے دیکھنے سے یقینی طور پر شناخت

کر سکتے کہ حضرت موسیٰ اور حضرت مسیح اور دوسرے گزشتہ نبی فی الحقیقت اسی پاک

اور مقدس جماعت میں سے ہیں جن کو خدا نے اپنے لطف خاص سے اپنی رسالت

کے لئے چن لیا ہے۔ یہ ہم کو فرقان مجید کا احسان ماننا چاہئے جس نے اپنی روشنی ہر

زمانہ میں آپ دکھلائی اور پھر اس کامل روشنی سے گزشتہ نبیوں کی صداقتیں بھی ہم پر

ظاہر کر دیں۔ اور یہ احسان نہ فقط ہم پر بلکہ آدم سے لے کر مسیح تک ان تمام نبیوں پر

ہے کہ جو قرآن شریف سے پہلے گزر چکے۔

(براہین احمدیہ حاشیہ در حاشیہ، روحانی خزائن جلد ۱ صفحہ 290)

29- We speak the truth and can never desist from doing so: had the Holy Prophet, may peace and blessings of Allah be upon him, not been raised and had the Holy Quran not been revealed, whose potent properties were witnessed by our elders and spiritual leaders in the past and we still witness today, it would have been very difficult for us, on the strength of Biblical account alone, to recognize Moses and Jesus and other earlier prophets to be belonging to that pious and righteous assembly of people whom God, out of His grace, had selected to be appointed as prophets. We must acknowledge this spiritual favour of the Holy Quran that it displays its light in every age and then with the help of that perfect light convinced us of the truth of earlier prophets. And this favour is not only shown unto us but is also shown unto all those prophets who appeared from the time of Adam to the time of Jesus (peace be upon them) prior to the advent of the Holy Quran.

(Braheen, e Ahrnadiyya, sub footnote: Roohani Khaza'in, Vol. 1, p. 290)

30- آج رُوئے زمین پر سب الہامی کتابوں میں سے ایک فرقان مجید ہی ہے کہ جس کا

کلام الٰہی ہونا دلائل قطعیہ سے ثابت ہے۔ جس کے اصول نجات کے بالکل راستی اور

وضع فطرتی پر مبنی ہیں ۔ جس کے عقائد ایسے کامل اور مستحکم ہیں جو براہین قویہ ان کی صداقت پر شاہدِ ناطق ہیں، جس کے احکام حق محض پر قائم ہیں، جس کی تعلیمات ہر یک طرح کی آمیزشِ شرک اور بدعت اور مخلوق پرستی سے بالکلّی پاک ہیں، جس میں توحید اور تعظیمِ الٰہی اور کمالاتِ حضرت عزّت کے ظاہر کرنے کے لئے انتہا کا جوش ہے، جس میں یہ خوبی ہے کہ سراسر وحدانیتِ جنابِ الٰہی سے بھرا ہوا ہے اور کسی طرح کا دھبہ، نقصان اور عیب اور نالائق صفات کا ذاتِ پاک حضرت باری تعالیٰ پر نہیں لگاتا اور کسی اعتقاد کو زبردستی تسلیم کرانا نہیں چاہتا بلکہ جو تعلیم دیتا ہے اس کی صداقت کی وجوہات پہلے دکھلا لیتا ہے اور ہر ایک مطلب اور مدّعا کو حجج اور براہین سے ثابت کرتا ہے ۔ اور ہر یک اصول کی حقیّت پر دلائل واضح بیان کر کے مرتبۂ یقین کامل اور معرفتِ تام تک پہنچاتا ہے ۔ اور جو خرابیاں اور ناپاکیاں اور خلل اور فساد لوگوں کے عقائد اور اعمال اور اقوال اور افعال میں پڑے ہوئے ہیں ان تمام مفاسد کو روشن براہین سے دور کرتا ہے اور وہ تمام آداب سکھاتا ہے کہ جن کا جاننا انسان کو انسان بننے کے لئے نہایت ضروری ہے اور ہر یک فساد کی اسی زور سے مدافعت کرتا ہے کہ جس زور سے وہ آج کل پھیلا ہوا ہے اس کی تعلیم نہایت مستقیم اور قوی اور سلیم ہے گویا احکامِ قدرتی کا ایک آئینہ ہے اور قانونِ فطرت کی ایک عکسی تصویر ہے اور بینائیِ دلی اور بصیرتِ قلبی کے لئے ایک آفتابِ چشم افروز ہے ۔

(براہین احمدیہ، روحانی خزائن جلد 1 صفحہ 81-82)

30-Of all the revealed Books which we find today, it is only the Holy Quran whose claim to having been revealed from God is established on the strength of irrefutable arguments. The principle it has enunciated regarding salvation corresponds exactly with the dictates of truth and human nature. The doctrines it propounds are so perfect and well founded that they are entirely supported by powerful and irrefutable evidence. Its injunctions are based on nothing but the truth. Its teachings are completely free from adulteration or idolatry, innovation and creature worship. It is a book in which there is exceeding eagerness to manifest the Oneness and Greatness of God and to emphasize the perfection of the attributes of the One and Only God. It is a Book which has this outstanding quality that it is filled entirely and purely with the teachings of the Unity of God and does not permit any manner of blemish or defect, or shortcoming or any other aspersion to be cast against the Holy Creator. It does not desire to impose any doctrine perforce. On the contrary, it precedes everything that it expounds with such arguments and logic as establish its truth. It proves its objectives and purport with weighty arguments and strong evidence. Having presented clear arguments to explain every principle it enunciates, it leads man to firm belief and absolute understanding of realities. It removes with the help of lucid enunciation, all the defects, impurities and irregularities which infest human beliefs, practices, words and deeds. It also teaches all etiquettes which are essential to cultivate human values in man. It meets the challenge of every corruption with no less a force than that displayed by the corruption itself prevalent in the world today. Its teachings are straight, powerful and well balanced as if they were a reflective mirror of nature itself and a true copy of the law of nature. It is like an enlightening sun for the inner eye and perceptive faculty of the heart.

(Braheen e Ahmadiyya: Roohani Khaza'in Vol. I, pp. 81-82)

۳۱؎ نور فرقاں ہے جو سب نوروں سے اُجلیٰ نکلا

پاک وہ جس سے یہ انوار کا دریا نکلا

حق کی توحید کا مرجھا ہی چلا تھا پودا

ناگہاں غیب سے یہ چشمۂ اَصفیٰ نکلا

یا الٰہی تیرا فرقاں ہے کہ اِک عالَم ہے

جو ضروری تھا وہ سب اِس میں مہیا نکلا

سب جہاں چھان چکے ساری دکانیں دیکھیں

مئے عرفاں کا یہی ایک ہی شیشہ نکلا

کس سے اس نور کی ممکن ہو جہاں میں تشبیہ

وہ تو ہر بات میں ہر وصف میں یکتا نکلا

پہلے سمجھے تھے کہ موسیٰ کا عصا ہے فرقاں

پھر جو سوچا تو ہر اک لفظ مسیحا نکلا

ہے قصور اپنا ہی اندھوں کا وگرنہ وہ نور

ایسا چمکا ہے کہ صد نیّر بیضا نکلا

زندگی ایسوں کی کیا خاک ہے اِس دنیا میں

جن کا اس نور کے ہوتے بھی دل اَعمیٰ نکلا

(براہین احمدیہ حاشیہ در حاشیہ، روحانی خزائن جلد ۱ صفحہ ۳۰۵-۳۰۶)

31-The light of the Holy Quran,

　　is a light more clear

　　and Bright, by far

　　than any other kind of light!

　　And holy, indeed, is He,

Who is the Source
of this veritable,
river of Radiance!

Of faith
in the Unity of God;
the plant indeed, had started
to wither away and die;
When, all of a sudden
this limpid spring
burst into being,
and began to flow!

O Lord!
Does Thy Word constitute
only a book? Or is it a universe
in itself? For, whatsoever
was indispensable for mankind,
for progress of the human mind
we find amply provided
in this marvellous Scripture!

Over the whole world,
I have let my thoughts range
in a diligent search;
And I have tried every shop
in the market place:
But of the wine of true
Gnosis, of true comprehension,
I have found but one single
flask!

It is not possible
to liken this light to anything:

For in everything, in every
quality, it stands alone –
absolutely unique!

There was a time
when we thought the Holy Quran
was alive, like the Staff
of Moses: but when we gave
a second thought to the matter,
we found that not only
was it alive in itself, every
single word in it had also
the life-giving quality
of a Messiah!

It is the fault of the blind themselves,
otherwise that light.
Is so intensely brilliant,
that it shines forth,
with the intensity
of a hundred suns.

Woe to the life of such,
on this Earth,
Who had access,
to this light.
But their hearts,
turned out to be blind.

(Braheen e Ahmadiyya, sub footnote: Roohani Khaza'in, Vol. 1, pg. 305-306)

۔32 اے عزیزو سنو کہ بے قرآں

حق کو ملتا نہیں کبھی انساں

دل میں ہر وقت نور بھرتا ہے

سینہ کو خوب صاف کرتا ہے

اس کے اَوصاف کیا کروں میں بیاں

وہ تو دیتا ہے جاں کو اَور اک جاں

وہ تو وہ چمکا ہے نیّر اکبر

اس سے انکار ہو سکے کیونکر

بحر حکمت ہے وہ کلام تمام

عشق حق کا پلا رہا ہے جام

دردمندوں کی ہے دوا وہی ایک

ہے خدا سے خدا نما وہی ایک

ہم نے پایا خور ہدی وہی ایک

ہم نے دیکھا ہے دلربا وہی ایک

اس کے منکر جو بات کہتے ہیں

یونہی اک واہیات کہتے ہیں

(براہین احمدیہ حاشیہ در حاشیہ، روحانی خزائن جلد 1 صفحہ 299-300)

32-Listen 0 those dear to me

   that without the Quran,

man can never reach the truth.

It ever fills the heart with light,

cleanses the bosom most thoroughly.

How can I acquit myself

in praising its qualities,
Lo! it bestows another life to this life.

Behold! It shines forth
like a sun at its zenith,
How can one ever deny its brilliance.

Every word of it is an ocean of wisdom
It makes one drink cups full of love of God.

That only is the one rescuer for sufferers
The only sign from God which leads to God.
That is the only sun of guidance we found,
That is the only
Captor of hearts we have ever seen.

Whatever they say who deny it,
Say nothing but sheer nonsense.

(Braheen e Ahmadiyya, Sub footnote: Roohani Khaza'in Vol. 1:, p 299-300)

THE MISSION OF THE PROMISED MESSIAH

(Peace be on him)

۳۳۔خواب میں دیکھا کہ لوگ ایک مُحیی کوتلاش کرتے پھرتے ہیں۔اورایک شخص اس عاجز کے سامنے آیااوراشارہ سے اس نے کہا هٰذَا رَجُلٌ یُحِبُّ رَسُوْلَ اللّٰه۔یعنی یہ وہ آدمی ہے جورسول اللہ سے محبت رکھتا ہے۔اوراس قول سے یہ مطلب تھا کہ شرطِ اعظم اس عہدہ کی محبت رسول ہے۔سووہ اس شخص میں متحقق ہے۔

(براہین احمدیہ حاشیہ درحاشیہ،روحانی خزائن جلد۱ صفحہ 598)

33-In a dream I saw that people were searching for a Rejuvenator. One of them came forward and pointing in my direction declared: 'This is the man who loves the Messenger of Allah.' By this they meant that the principal qualification which the destined Rejuvenator had to possess was the love of the Holy Prophet, may peace and blessings of Allah be upon him. And according to them, I most certainly fulfilled this condition.

(Braheen e Ahmadiyya, sub footnote: Roohani Khaza'in Vol. 1 p. 598

۳۴۔دنیا مجھے قبول نہیں کرسکتی کیونکہ مَیں دنیا میں سے نہیں ہوں۔مگرجن کی فطرت کواُس عالَم کا حصّہ دیا گیا ہے وہ مجھے قبول کرتے ہیں اورکریں گے۔جو مجھے چھوڑتا ہے وہ اُس کو چھوڑتا ہے جس نے مجھے بھیجا ہے اور جو مجھ سے پیوند کرتا ہے وہ اُس سے کرتا ہے جس کی طرف سے مَیں آیا ہوں۔میرے ہاتھ میں ایک چراغ ہے جو شخص میرے پاس آتا ہے ضرور وہ اُس روشنی سے حصّہ لے گا مگر جو شخص وہم اور بدگمانی سے دُور بھاگتا ہے وہ ظلمت میں ڈال دیا جائے گا۔اس زمانہ کا حصنِ حصین مَیں ہوں جو مجھ

34- The world cannot accept me, because I do not belong to this world. But those who are gifted with a measure of other worldliness are the ones who accept and will accept me. The one who rejects me rejects Him Who has sent me, and the one who is grafted to me is grafted to Him Whom I represent. I bear a torch which will illumine all those who come close to me, but the one who entertains suspicion and doubt and runs away will be subjected to darkness. I am the impregnable fortress for this age; whoever enters my fold will be protected from thieves, robbers and the beasts of the wilderness. *(Fatah Islam: Roohani Khaza'in Vol. 3, p. 34)*

35- I call to witness God Almighty, Who holds my life in His hand, that compared to every other soul, He has gifted me with overwhelmingly greater ability and access to the understanding and the deeper wisdom of the Holy Quran. If any of the Maulvis (traditional Muslim scholars) who oppose me in response to my repeated invitations had attempted to outshine me in the exposition of the Holy Quran, God would have most certainly frustrated his attempts and exposed his ignorance. Hence, the understanding of the Quran which has been granted me is a Sign of Allah, the Glorious, and I have full trust in Allah's grace that soon the world will begin to see that I am true in this claim.   *(Siraj-e-Muneer: Roohani Khaza'in Vol. 12, p. 41)*

۳۶۔مَیں اکیلا نہیں وہ مولیٰ کریم میرے ساتھ ہے اور کوئی اس سے بڑھ کر مجھ سے قریب تر نہیں۔ اسی کے فضل سے مجھ کو یہ عاشقانہ روح ملی ہے کہ دکھا اٹھا کر بھی اس کے دین کیلئے خدمت بجا لاؤں اور اسلامی مہمّات کو بشوق وصدق تمام تر انجام دوں۔اس کام پراس نے آپ نے مجھے مامور کیا ہے اب کسی کے کہنے سے مَیں نہیں رک سکتا۔   (آئینہ کمالات اسلام،روحانی خزائن جلد۵ صفحہ ۳۵)

36-I am not alone. That noble Lord is with me. No one could be closer to me than Him. It is only by His Grace that I have been granted a loving soul, ever willing to serve His cause in the face of suffering; so that I should render with zeal and sincerity, outstanding services in the cause of the faith and carry out to victory, great (spiritual) expeditions for Islam. He has commissioned me to accomplish all this, and none can make me desist from pursuing this cause.

(Ayena e Kamalat e Islam: Roohani Khaza'in Vol. 5, p 35)

۳۷۔ایک تقویٰ شعار آدمی کے لئے یہ کافی تھا کہ خدا نے مجھے مفتریوں کی طرح ہلاک نہیں کیا بلکہ میرے ظاہر اور باطن اور میرے جسم اور میری روح پر وہ احسان کئے جن کو مَیں شمار نہیں کر سکتا۔مَیں جوان تھا جب خدا کی وحی اور الہام کا دعویٰ کیا اور اب مَیں بوڑھا ہو گیا اور ابتداء دعویٰ پر بیس برس سے بھی زیادہ عرصہ گزر گیا۔بہت سے میرے دوست اور عزیز جو مجھ سے چھوٹے تھے فوت ہو گئے اور مجھے اُس نے عمر دراز بخشی اور

ہر ایک مشکل میں میرا متکفّل اور متولّی رہا۔ پس کیا ان لوگوں کے یہی نشان ہوا کرتے ہیں کہ جو خدا تعالیٰ پر افترا باندھتے ہیں ۔ (انجام آتھم،روحانی خزائن جلد 11 صفحہ 50-51)

37-It should have sufficed a righteous person to observe that God showered such blessings, internally and externally, upon my body and my soul that I cannot keep count of them. I was young when I claimed to be the recipient of Divine revelation. Now I have become old. More than twenty years have passed since the beginning of my claim. Many dear friends younger than I have passed away but He has granted me this ripe old age. He remained my Mentor and He alone is Sufficient to help me out of all predicaments. Tell me, are these the characteristics of those who falsely impute things to Allah? *(Anjam e Atham: Roohani Khaza'in Vol. 11, p. 50-51)*

38۔ مسیح موعود کا آسمان سے اُترنا محض جھوٹا خیال ہے ۔ یاد رکھو کہ کوئی آسمان سے نہیں اُترے گا۔ ہمارے سب مخالف جواب زندہ موجود ہیں وہ تمام مریں گے اور کوئی اُن میں سے عیسیٰؑ بن مریم کو آسمان سے اُترتے نہیں دیکھے گا۔ اور پھر ان کی اولاد جو باقی رہے گی وہ بھی مرے گی اور اُن میں سے بھی کوئی آدمی عیسیٰؑ بن مریم کو آسمان سے اُترتے نہیں دیکھے گا۔ اور پھر اولاد کی اولاد مرے گی اور وہ بھی مریم کے بیٹے کو آسمان سے اُترتے نہیں دیکھے گی۔ تب خدا اُن کے دلوں میں گھبراہٹ ڈالے گا کہ زمانہ صلیب کے غلبہ کا بھی گزر گیا اور دنیا دوسرے رنگ میں آ گئی مگر مریم کا بیٹا عیسیٰؑ اب تک آسمان سے نہ اُترا۔ تب دانشمند یک دفعہ اس عقیدہ سے بیزار ہو جائیں گے۔ اور ابھی تیسری صدی آج کے دن سے پوری نہیں ہوگی کہ عیسیٰؑ کے انتظار کرنے والے کیا مسلمان اور کیا عیسائی سخت نومید اور بدظن ہو کر اس جھوٹے عقیدہ کو چھوڑیں گے اور

دنیا میں ایک ہی مذہب ہوگا اور ایک ہی پیشوا۔ مَیں تو ایک تخم ریزی کرنے آیا ہوں سو میرے ہاتھ سے وہ تخم بویا گیا اور اب وہ بڑھے گا اور پھولے گا اور کوئی نہیں جو اُس کو روک سکے۔

(تذکرۃ الشہادتین، روحانی خزائن جلد 20 صفحہ 67)

38-Remember very well that no one shall ever come down from heaven. All our opponents who live today shall die and none from them shall ever see Jesus son of Mary coming down from heaven; then their children that are left after them shall also die and none from among them shall ever see Jesus son of Mary coming down from heaven and then their third generation shall also die and they too shall not see the son of Mary coming down. Then God shall cause great consternation in their minds and they shall then say that the period of the dominance of the cross has also passed away and the way of life has changed completely, yet the son of Mary has not come down. Then in dismay the wise among them shall forsake this belief and three centuries from now shall not have passed when those who await the coming of Jesus son of Mary, whether they be Muslims or Christians, shall relinquish altogether this conception. Then shall prevail only one religion over the whole world and there shall be only one religious Leader. I came only to sow the seed which has been planted by my hand. It shall now grow and flourish and there is none who can hinder it.

(Tazkiratush Shahadatain: Roohani Khaza'in Vol. 20, p. 67)

THE OBJECTIVES OF

FOUNDING THE COMMUNITY

۳۹۔اے میرے دوستو! جو میرے سلسلہ بیعت میں داخل ہو خدا ہمیں اور تمہیں اُن باتوں کی توفیق دے جن سے وہ راضی ہو جائے۔ آج تم تھوڑے ہو اور تحقیر کی نظر سے دیکھے گئے ہو اور ایک ابتلا کا وقت تم پر ہے اسی سُنّت اللہ کے موافق جو قدیم سے جاری ہے۔ ہر ایک طرف سے کوشش ہوگی کہ تم ٹھوکر کھاؤ اور تم ہر طرح سے ستائے جاؤ گے اور طرح طرح کی باتیں تمہیں سُننی پڑیں گی اور ہر ایک جو تمہیں زبان یا ہاتھ سے دکھ دے گا وہ خیال کرے گا کہ اسلام کی حمایت کر رہا ہے۔ اور کچھ آسمانی ابتلا بھی تم پر آئیں گے تا تم ہر طرح سے آزمائے جاؤ۔ سو تم اس وقت سُن رکھو کہ تمہارے فتح مند اور غالب ہو جانے کی یہ راہ نہیں کہ تم اپنی خشک منطق سے کام لو یا تمسخر کے مقابل پر تمسخر کی باتیں کرو۔ یا گالی کے مقابل پر گالی دو۔ کیونکہ اگر تم نے یہی راہیں اختیار کیں تو تمہارے دل سخت ہو جائیں گے اور تم میں صرف باتیں ہی باتیں ہوں گی جن سے خدا تعالیٰ نفرت کرتا ہے اور کراہت کی نظر سے دیکھتا ہے۔ سو تم ایسا نہ کرو کہ اپنے پر دو لعنتیں جمع کر لو، ایک خَلقت کی اور دوسری خدا کی بھی۔

(ازالہ اوہام، روحانی خزائن جلد 3 صفحہ 546-547)

39-O my friends, who have entered into a covenant with me, may God enable me and enable you to do such things as would please Him. Today, you are small in number and are being treated with contempt. You are passing through a great period of trial. According to His established scheme of things, it was decreed by God since time immemorial that efforts would be made from all directions that you should falter. You will be harassed in every way and you will have to bear with all manners of talk. Each one of those who will inflict misery upon you with his tongue or with his hand will do it in the belief that he is doing it in the service of Islam. So also will you be tried from Heaven so that you are tried in every possible way. Hearken ye, therefore, that for you the road to victory does not lie in the direction of dry logic which you may employ or that you should return mockery for mockery or that you should return abuse for abuse. If you adopt such a course your hearts will become hardened and you will be left with nothing but mere words which God Almighty loathes and looks down upon with aversion. So do not behave in a manner whereby you should become subject to two curses, the curse of men and the curse of God.

(Izala e Auham: Roohani Khaza'in Vol. 3, pp. 546 -547)

۴۰۔ یہ مت خیال کرو کہ خدا تمہیں ضائع کر دے گا۔ تم خدا کے ہاتھ کا ایک بیج ہو جو زمین میں بویا گیا۔ خدا فرماتا ہے کہ یہ بیج بڑھے گا اور پھولے گا اور ہر ایک طرف سے اس کی شاخیں نکلیں گی اور ایک بڑا درخت ہو جائے گا۔ پس مبارک وہ جو خدا کی بات پر ایمان رکھے اور درمیان میں آنے والے ابتلاؤں سے نہ ڈرے کیونکہ ابتلاؤں کا آنا بھی ضروری ہے تا خدا تمہاری آزمائش کرے کہ کون اپنے دعویٰ بیعت میں صادق اور کون کاذب ہے۔ وہ جو کسی ابتلا سے لغزش کھائے گا وہ کچھ بھی خدا کا نقصان نہیں کرے گا اور بدبختی اُس کو جہنم تک پہنچائے گی۔ اگر وہ پیدا نہ ہوتا تو اُس کے لئے اچھا تھا۔ مگر وہ سب لوگ جو خیر تک صبر کریں گے اور اُن پر مصائب کے زلزلے آ ئیں گے اور حوادث کی آندھیاں چلیں گی اور قوم میں ہنسی اور ٹھٹھا کریں گی اور دنیا اُن سے سخت کراہت کے ساتھ پیش آئے گی وہ آخر فتح یاب ہوں گے اور برکتوں کے دروازے اُن پر کھولے جائیں گے۔ خدا نے مجھے مخاطب کر کے فرمایا کہ میں اپنی

40-Never think for a moment that God will let you go to waste; you are indeed a seed planted by the very hand of God in the soil. Thus, declares God, this seed will sprout and grow and will branch out in every direction and will turn into a mighty tree. So, blessed be he who has trust in the word of God and should fear not the intervening trials. Remember that it is essential for trials to come so that thereby, Allah may distinguish which of you is true in his covenant of Bai'at and which of you is false. He who stumbles in the course of any trial will not harm God in the least and his evil fate will lead him ultimately to hell. Would that he were not born. As for those who remain steadfast to the end, however much they have been confronted with calamities and have passed through periods of great shaking and trepidations, those who have been subjected to mockery and are laughed at by nations, and whom the world will treat with utter disdain, they are the ones who will emerge victorious in the end, and the gates of blessings will be thrown open to welcome them. Thus has God instructed me as He spoke to me that I make it clear to my followers that such among men who have believed and their faith has no trace of worldly motives nor is it blemished with cowardice and hypocrisy, theirs is a faith which never fails to comply with the requirements of obedience at any level. Such are the people endeared by God. It is about them that God declares that they tread the path of truth.

(Al Wasiyyat: Roohani Khaza'in Vol. 20, p. 309)

۴۱۔ ناانصافی پر ضد کر کے سچائی کا خون نہ کرو۔ حق کو قبول کر لو اگرچہ ایک بچہ سے۔ اور اگر مخالف کی طرف حق پاؤ تو پھر فی الفور اپنی خشک منطق کو چھوڑ دو۔ سچ پر ٹھہر جاؤ اور سچی گواہی دو۔ جیسا کہ اللہ جلّ شانَہٗ فرماتا ہے: فَاجْتَنِبُوا الرِّجْسَ مِنَ الْاَوْثَانِ وَاجْتَنِبُوْا قَوْلَ الزُّوْرِ (سورۃ الحج:31) یعنی بتوں کی پلیدی سے بچو اور جھوٹ سے بھی کہ وہ بُت سے کم نہیں۔ جو چیز قبلۂ حق سے تمہارا مُنہ پھیرتی ہے وہی تمہاری راہ میں بُت ہے۔ سچی گواہی دو اگرچہ تمہارے باپوں یا بھائیوں یا دوستوں پر ہو۔ چاہئے کہ کوئی عداوت بھی تمہیں انصاف سے مانع نہ ہو۔ باہم بخل اور کینہ اور حسد اور بُغض اور بے مہری چھوڑ دو اور ایک ہو جاؤ۔ قرآن شریف کے بڑے حکم دو ہی ہیں۔ ایک توحید ومحبت واطاعت باری عزّ اسمُہٗ۔ دوسری ہمدردی اپنے بھائیوں اور اپنے بنی نوع کی۔

(ازالہ اوہام، روحانی خزائن جلد 3 صفحہ 550)

41-Slay not truth by sticking obstinately to injustice. Accept the truth though you receive it from a child. Similarly, when you find your enemy to be in the right, renounce your dry argumentation forthwith. Adhere firmly to truth and bear true witness. Remember how the Glorious God admonishes you:

فَاجْتَنِبُوا الرِّجْسَ مِنَ الْاَوْثَانِ وَاجْتَنِبُوْا قَوْلَ الزُّوْرِ

This means, shun the abomination of idols and stay away from the telling of lies which is no less sinful than idolatry. Anything which turns you away from your true goal, that is an idol in your path. Bear true witness even if it should be against your fathers or brothers or friends. Do not let enmity against anyone prevent you from dispensing justice. Treat not one another with miserliness, show no rancour, entertain no jealousy and be not cold hearted. The teachings of the Holy Quran can be divided into two major categories. The first being Unity of God and love and obedience to Him, exalted be His name. The second is to treat kindly, your brothers and fellow beings.

(Izala e Auham, Pt. 2: Roohani Khaza'in Vol. 3, p.550)

۴۲۔ سچائی اختیار کرو۔ سچائی اختیار کرو کہ وہ دیکھ رہا ہے کہ تمہارے دل کیسے ہیں ۔ کیا
انسان اُس کو بھی دھوکہ دے سکتا ہے؟ کیا اس کے آگے بھی مکّاریاں پیش جاتی ہیں؟

(ازالہ اوہام، روحانی خزائن جلد 3 صفحہ 549)

42-Abide by the truth and hold fast to it. He sees what is in
your hearts. Can man ever deceive Him? Can trickery be of
any avail against Him?

(Izala e Auham, Pt. 2: Roohani Khaza'in Vol. 3, p. 549')

۴۳۔ تم اگر چاہتے ہو کہ آسمان پر تم سے خدا راضی ہو تو تم باہم ایسے ایک ہو جاؤ جیسے ایک
پیٹ میں سے دو بھائی۔ تم میں سے زیادہ بزرگ وہی ہے جو زیادہ اپنے بھائی کے گناہ
بخشتا ہے۔ اور بد بخت ہے وہ جو ضد کرتا ہے اور نہیں بخشتا۔ سو اس کا مجھ میں حصہ نہیں۔
خدا کی لعنت سے بہت خائف رہو کہ وہ قدّوس اور غیور ہے ۔ بدکار خدا کا قرب
حاصل نہیں کر سکتا۔ متکبّر اُس کا قرب حاصل نہیں کر سکتا۔ ظالم اُس کا قرب حاصل
نہیں کر سکتا خائن اُس کا قرب حاصل نہیں کر سکتا۔ اور ہر ایک جو اُس کے نام کے لئے
غیرت مند نہیں اُس کا قرب حاصل نہیں کر سکتا۔ وہ جو دنیا پر کتّوں یا چیونٹیوں یا
گِدّوں کی طرح گرتے ہیں اور دنیا سے آرام یافتہ ہیں وہ اُس کا قرب حاصل نہیں
کر سکتے ۔ ہر ایک ناپاک آنکھ اُس سے دور ہے ۔ ہر ایک ناپاک دل اُس سے بے خبر
ہے۔ وہ جو اُس کے لئے آگ میں ہے وہ آگ سے نجات دیا جائے گا۔ وہ جو اُس
کے لئے روتا ہے وہ ہنسے گا۔ وہ جو اُس کے لئے دنیا سے ٹوٹتا ہے وہ اُس کو ملے گا۔ تم
سچے دل سے اور پورے صدق سے اور سرگرمی کے قدم سے خدا کے دوست بنو تا وہ
بھی تمہارا دوست بن جائے ۔ تم ماتحتوں پر اور اپنی بیویوں پر اور اپنے غریب
بھائیوں پر رحم کرو تا آسمان پر تم پر بھی رحم ہو۔ تم سچ مچ اُس کے ہو جاؤ تا وہ بھی تمہارا

ہوجاوے۔

(کشتی نوح، روحانی خزائن جلد ۱۹ صفحہ ۱۲-۱۳)

43- If you want that God should be pleased with you in heaven, unite and be one like two brothers of the same mother. Nobler is he among you who forgives the sins of his brother more than others and doomed is he who is stubborn and does not forgive. He has nothing in common with me. Live in fear, lest you be cursed by God. He is Holy and He is a jealous Guardian over the honour of His beloved ones. The wicked cannot attain His nearness, the arrogant cannot gain His nearness, nor can the tyrant nor the one who breaks trust. Nor can he, who is not ready to lay down everything for the honour of His name, nor those who fall to the pleasures of the world like dogs and ants and vultures and who are comfortable with the luxuries of the world. Each unchaste eye is remote from Him, each impure heart knows Him not. Those who remain in agony for His cause will be delivered from the fire of hell. He who weeps for Him will laugh at last and he who breaks away from the world for His sake will meet Him. Be Allah's friend with all your heart, in all sincerity, gaining His nearness with ever growing zeal. Be kind to your subordinates, to your wives and to your less fortunate brothers so that you may be shown kindness in heaven. Become truly His so that He may belong to you.

(Kashti e Nuh: Roohani Khaza'in Vol. 19, pp. 12,13)

۴۴۔ سوائے وے تمام لوگو! جو اپنے تئیں میری جماعت شمار کرتے ہو آسمان پر تم اُس وقت میری جماعت شمار کئے جاؤ گے جب سچ سچ تقویٰ کی راہوں پر قدم مارو گے۔ سو اپنی پنج وقتہ نمازوں کو ایسے خوف اور حضور سے ادا کرو کہ گویا تم خدا تعالیٰ کو دیکھتے ہو اور

اپنے روزوں کو خدا کے لئے صدق کے ساتھ پورے کرو۔ ہر ایک جو زکوٰۃ کے لائق
ہے وہ زکوٰۃ دے اور جس پر حج فرض ہو چکا ہے اور کوئی مانع نہیں وہ حج کرے۔ نیکی کو
سنوار کر ادا کرو اور بدی کو بیزار ہو کر ترک کرو۔ یقیناً یاد رکھو کہ کوئی عمل خدا تک نہیں
پہنچ سکتا جو تقویٰ سے خالی ہے۔ ہر ایک نیکی کی جڑ تقویٰ ہے۔ جس عمل میں یہ جڑ
ضائع نہیں ہوگی وہ عمل بھی ضائع نہیں ہوگا۔ ضرور ہے کہ انواع رنج و مصیبت سے
تمہارا امتحان بھی ہو جیسا کہ پہلے مومنوں کے امتحان ہوئے۔ سو خبردار رہو ایسا نہ ہو کہ
ٹھوکر کھاؤ۔ زمین تمہارا کچھ بھی بگاڑ نہیں سکتی اگر تمہارا آسمان سے پختہ تعلق ہے۔
جب کبھی تم اپنا نقصان کرو گے تو اپنے ہاتھوں سے، نہ دشمن کے ہاتھوں سے۔ اگر
تمہاری زمینی عزت ساری جاتی رہے تو خدا تمہیں ایک لازوال عزت آسمان پر دے
گا سو تم اس کو مت چھوڑو۔ اور ضرور ہے کہ تم دکھ دیئے جاؤ اور اپنی کئی امیدوں سے
بے نصیب کئے جاؤ۔ سو اِن صورتوں سے تم دلگیر مت ہو کیونکہ تمہارا خدا تمہیں آزماتا
ہے کہ تم اس کی راہ میں ثابت قدم ہو یا نہیں۔ اگر تم چاہتے ہو کہ آسمان پر فرشتے بھی
تمہاری تعریف کریں تو تم مار میں کھاؤ اور خوش رہو اور گالیاں سنو اور شکر کرو اور نا کامیاں
دیکھو اور پیوند مت توڑو۔ تم خدا کی آخری جماعت ہو سو وہ عمل نیک دکھلاؤ جو اپنے
کمال میں انتہائی درجہ پر ہو۔

(کشتئ نوح، روحانی خزائن جلد 19 صفحہ 15)

44-So listen all you who consider yourselves to be of my
community. When you truly tread the path of righteousness,
only then will you be counted in heaven as my community. So
perform your prayers five times a day inspired by such awe
and awareness of the presence of Almighty God as if you were
seeing Him with your own eyes. Also observe the days of fast
sincerely for the sake of Allah, fulfilling their requirements. Each
one of you who is assessable to Zakat, should pay Zakat.
Similarly anyone upon whom Pilgrimage has become obligatory

and has no cause for exemption must perform the Pilgrimage. Do good deeds in the best of manners and reject evil with repugnance. Remember that no deed of yours which is devoid of righteousness will be ever entertained by God. An act of goodness is only that which is rooted in the fear of God. No act in which this root remains intact will be permitted to go to waste. It is inevitable that you should be tried with diverse trials of pain and misfortune as the faithful before you were tried. So remain always wary lest you should stumble. The earth can do you no harm as long as you have firm ties with heaven. If ever you come to grief, you will come to grief at your own hands rather than at the hands of your enemies. If you lose all honour on this earth, God will bestow an eternal honour upon you in heaven. So leave Him not. You are bound to suffer pain at their hands and you will be deprived of the fulfilment of many of your aspirations. But be not heavy hearted; God merely tries you whether you are steadfast in His cause or not. If you desire that even angels should praise you in heaven then suffer in the path of Allah with grace and remain cheerful. Hear abuse and remain grateful and despite frustration break not your ties (with God). You are the last people raised by God so do such deeds of piety as touch the loftiest standards of excellence.

(Kashti Nuh: Roohani Khaza'in Vol. 19, p.15)

ADMONITIONS

۴۵۔مَیں اپنی جماعت کو نصیحت کرتا ہوں کہ تکبّر سے بچو کیونکہ تکبّر ہمارے خداوند ذوالجلال کی آنکھوں میں سخت مکروہ ہے۔ مگر تم شاید نہیں سمجھو گے کہ تکبّر کیا چیز ہے۔ پس مُجھ سے سمجھ لو کہ مَیں خدا کی رُوح سے بولتا ہوں۔ ہر ایک شخص جو اپنے بھائی کو اِس لئے حقیر جانتا ہے کہ وہ اس سے زیادہ عالم یا زیادہ عقلمند یا زیادہ ہُنر مند ہے وہ متکبّر ہے کیونکہ وہ خدا کو سرچشمہ عقل اور علم کا نہیں سمجھتا اور اپنے تئیں کچھ چیز قرار دیتا ہے۔ کیا خدا قادر نہیں کہ اُس کو دیوانہ کر دے اور اُس کے اُس بھائی کو جس کو وہ چھوٹا سمجھتا ہے اُس سے بہتر عقل اور علم اور ہُنر دے دے۔ ایسا ہی وہ شخص جو اپنے کسی مال یا جاہ و حشمت کا تصوّر کر کے اپنے بھائی کو حقیر سمجھتا ہے وہ بھی متکبّر ہے کیونکہ وہ اِس بات کو بُھول گیا ہے کہ یہ جاہ و حشمت خدا نے ہی اُس کو دی تھی اور وہ اندھا ہے اور وہ نہیں جانتا کہ وہ خدا قادر ہے کہ اُس پر ایک ایسی گردش نازل کرے کہ وہ ایک دم میں اسفل السافلین میں جا پڑے اور اُس کے اُس بھائی کو جس کو وہ حقیر سمجھتا ہے اُس سے بہتر مال و دولت عطا کر دے۔ ایسا ہی وہ شخص جو اپنی صحت بدنی پر غرور کرتا ہے یا اپنے حسن اور جمال اور قوت اور طاقت پر نازاں ہے اور اپنے بھائی کا ٹھٹھے اور استہزا سے حقارت آمیز نام رکھتا ہے اور اُس کے بدنی عیوب لوگوں کو سُناتا ہے وہ بھی متکبّر ہے اور وہ اُس خدا سے بے خبر ہے کہ ایک دم میں اُس پر ایسے بدنی عیوب نازل کرے کہ اُس بھائی سے اُس کو بدتر کر دے۔ (نزول المسیح، روحانی خزائن جلد ۱۸ صفحہ ۴۰۲)

45-I admonish my community to shun arrogance because arrogance is most loathsome to God, the Lord of Glory. You may not perhaps fully realize what arrogance is. So learn it from me because I speak with the spirit of God. Everyone who looks down upon his brother because he considers himself to be more learned, wiser, or more accomplished than him is arrogant. He is arrogant because, instead of considering God to be the Fountainhead of all wisdom and knowledge, he considers himself something. Does God not have the power to derange him mentally and instead grant superior knowledge, wisdom and dexterity to his brother whom he considers inferior? Likewise he too is arrogant who, thinking of his wealth or high status, looks down upon his brother. He is arrogant because he has ignored the fact that this status and grandeur were bestowed upon him by God. He is blind and does not realize that God has power to afflict him with such misfortune as, all of a sudden he is cast to the lowest of the low; and again He has the power to bestow greater wealth and prosperity upon that brother of his whom he considers small. Yet again, that person is arrogant who is proud of his superior bodily health, or of his handsomeness, or good looks, or strength, or prowess, and scornfully makes fun of his brother and teases him and addresses him with derisive names; not satisfied with this he advertises his physical defects. It is so because he is unaware of the existence of a God Who possesses power to suddenly inflict him with such bodily defects as may leave him much worse than his brother.

(Nuzul-ul-Masih: Roohani Khaza'in Vol. 18, p. 402)

46۔ اور چاہئے کہ تم بھی ہمدردی اور اپنے نفسوں کے پاک کرنے سے روح القدس سے حصہ لو کہ بجز روح القدس کے حقیقی تقویٰ حاصل نہیں ہوسکتی اور نفسانی جذبات کو بکلّی چھوڑ کر خدا کی رضا کے لئے وہ راہ اختیار کرو جو اُس سے زیادہ کوئی راہ تنگ نہ ہو۔ دنیا کی لذتوں پر فریفتہ مت ہو کہ وہ خدا سے جدا کرتی ہیں۔ اور خدا کے لئے تلخی کی زندگی

اختیار کرو۔ درد جس سے خدا راضی ہو اُس لذّت سے بہتر ہے جس سے خدا ناراض ہو
جائے۔ اور وہ شکست جس سے خدا راضی ہو اُس فتح سے بہتر ہے جو موجب غضب
الٰہی ہو۔ اُس محبت کو چھوڑ دو جو خدا کے غضب کے قریب کے کرے۔ اگر تم صاف دل
ہو کر اُس کی طرف آ جاؤ تو ہر ایک راہ میں وہ تمہاری مدد کرے گا اور کوئی دشمن تمہیں
نقصان نہیں پہنچا سکے گا۔   (الوصیت، روحانی خزائن جلد 20 صفحہ 307)

46-It is proper for you to have sympathy for others and to purify yourselves so that thereby you may share to a degree the qualities of the Holy Spirit. Remember that without the Holy Spirit true righteousness cannot be attained. Discard altogether the base animal desires in you and follow the path to the pleasure of Allah, be it the narrowest and most difficult of all. Do not be enamoured of worldly pleasures, because they lead you away from God. That suffering which pleases God is better than that pleasure which displeases Him. That defeat which pleases God is better than the victory which earns His displeasure. Abandon that love which draws you nigh to the wrath of Allah. If you come to Him with a pure heart, He will help you in every way and no enemy will be able to harm you.

(Al Wasiyyat: Roohani Khaza'in Vol. 20, p. 307)

47۔ لِبَاسُ التَّقْوٰی قرآن شریف کا لفظ ہے۔ یہ اِس بات کی طرف اشارہ ہے کہ روحانی
خوبصورتی اور روحانی زینت تقویٰ سے ہی پیدا ہوتی ہے۔ اور تقویٰ یہ ہے کہ انسان
خدا کی تمام اَمانتوں اور ایمانی عہد اور ایسا ہی مخلوق کی تمام اَمانتوں اور عہد کی حتی الوسع
رعایت رکھے یعنی ان کے دقیق درقیق پہلوؤں پر تا بمقدور کاربند ہو جائے۔
(براہین احمدیہ حصہ پنجم، روحانی خزائن جلد 21 صفحہ 210)

The attire of righteousness is a term of the Holy Quran. This points to the fact that spiritual beauty and spiritual adornment can only be achieved through righteousness. And righteousness means that a person should, to the best of his ability, discharge his responsibilities regarding his faculties and covenant of faith with God as a sacred trust. Also he should pay full regard to what he owes to his fellow human beings and to all that is created by God as a trust imposed on him. He should tread the path of righteousness to the minutest detail according to the best of his ability.

(Braheen e Ahmadiyya, Pt. 5: Roohani Khaza'in Vol. 21, p. 210)

THINKING ILL OF OTHERS

۴۸۔ بدظنّی ایک سخت بلا ہے جو ایمان کو ایسی جلدی جلا دیتی ہے جیسا کہ آتشِ سوزاں خس وخاشاک کو۔ اور وہ جو خدا کے مُرسَلوں پر بدظنّی کرتا ہے خدا اُس کا خود دشمن ہو جاتا ہے اور اس کی جنگ کے لئے کھڑا ہوتا ہے اور وہ اپنے برگزیدوں کے لئے اس قدر غیرت رکھتا ہے جو کسی میں اُس کی نظیر نہیں پائی جاتی۔ میرے پر جب طرح طرح کے حملے ہوئے تو وہی خدا کی غیرت میرے لئے برافروختہ ہوئی۔

(الوصیت، روحانی خزائن جلد 20 صفحہ 317 حاشیہ)

48-To think ill and attribute wrong motives to others' actions is a diseased and distorted attitude in man which destroys the quality of his faith and righteousness and consumes it as rapidly as blazing fire consumes tinder. When such diseased people make prophets of God the target of their insinuations and think ill of them, God becomes their enemy and stands up in defence of His prophets. He guards the honour of His dear ones with such jealousy as is unparalleled. When I was maligned and assailed in different ways, the same protective jealousy of God became operative in my defence.

(Al Wasiyyat, footnote: Roohani Khaza'in Vol. 20, p. 317)

۴۹۔ ''میں سچ کہتا ہوں کہ بدظنّی بہت ہی بری بلا ہے جو انسان کے ایمان کو تباہ کر دیتی ہے اور صدق اور راستی سے دور پھینک دیتی ہے اور دوستوں کو دشمن بنا دیتی ہے۔ صدیقوں کے کمال حاصل کرنے کے لئے ضروری ہے کہ انسان بدظنّی سے بہت ہی بچے اور اگر کسی کی نسبت کوئی سُوءِ ظن پیدا ہو تو کثرت کے ساتھ استغفار کرے اور

خدا تعالیٰ سے دعائیں کرے تاکہ اس معصیت اور اس کے بُرے نتیجہ سے بچ جاوے جو اس بدظنّی کے پیچھے آنے والا ہے۔ اس کو کبھی معمولی چیز نہیں سمجھنا چاہئے۔ یہ بہت ہی خطرناک بیماری ہے جس سے انسان بہت جلد ہلاک ہو جاتا ہے''۔

(ملفوظات جلد اول صفحہ 356)

49-I tell you truly that the habit of thinking ill of others is a great affliction which destroys a person's faith, flings him away from truth and turns his friends into foes. In order to attain the excellent virtues of a Siddeeq (Siddeeq is a term used by the Holy Quran indicating a spiritual rank next to that of prophets) it is necessary that a person should altogether shun the habit of thinking ill of others. If inadvertently he happens to have thought ill of others, he should forthwith repent and seek forgiveness repeatedly and pray to God that he may be protected from committing this folly again and be saved from its consequences. This spiritual malady should not be taken lightly. It is a highly dangerous disease which speedily destroys its victim.

(Malfoozat Vol. 1: p 356)

OUR TENETS

۵۰۔ ہمارے مذہب کا خلاصہ اور لُبّ لباب یہ ہے کہ لَاۤ اِلٰہ اِلَّا اللّٰهُ مُحَمَّدٌ رَّسُوۡلُ اللّٰهِ ہمارا اعتقاد جو ہم اس دنیوی زندگی میں رکھتے ہیں جس کے ساتھ ہم بفضل و توفیق باری تعالٰی اس عالَم گذران سے کوچ کریں گے یہ ہے کہ حضرت سیّدنا و مولانا محمد مصطفٰی صلی اللہ علیہ وسلم خاتم النّبیّین وخیرالمُرسَلین ہیں جن کے ہاتھ سے اکمال دین ہو چکا اور وہ نعمت بمرتبہ اتمام پہنچ چکی جس کے ذریعہ سے انسان راہ راست کو اختیار کر کے خدائے تعالٰی تک پہنچ سکتا ہے۔ اور ہم پختہ یقین کے ساتھ اس بات پر ایمان رکھتے ہیں کہ قرآن شریف خاتم کتب سماوی ہے اور ایک شُعبہ یا نقطہ اس کی شرائع اور حدود و احکام اور اوامر سے زیادہ نہیں ہو سکتا اور نہ کم ہو سکتا ہے۔ اور اب کوئی ایسی وحی یا ایسا الہام منجانب اللہ نہیں ہو سکتا جو احکام فرقانی کی ترمیم یا تنسیخ یا کسی ایک حکم کے تبدیل یا تغییر کر سکتا ہو۔ اگر کوئی ایسا خیال کرے تو وہ ہمارے نزدیک جماعت مومنین سے خارج اور مُلحد اور کافر ہے۔ (ازالہ اوہام، روحانی خزائن جلد ۳ صفحہ ۱۶۹-۱۷۰)

15- Gist of our faith is:

لَاۤ اِلٰہ اِلَّا اللّٰهُ مُحَمَّدٌ رَّسُوۡلُ اللّٰهِ

La Ilaha Illallah Muhammadur Rasulullah. (There is no god but Allah, Muhammad is the Messenger of Allah.) Our belief, which we hold in this life here on earth and to which we will continue to adhere firmly till the time that we pass on to the next world, is that our spiritual leader and master, Muhammad, peace and blessings of Allah be on him, is the Seal of the Prophets and the Best of the Messengers. At his hands religion has been perfected and blessing of Allah has been consummated which lead man to the right path and further on to God Himself. We hold this positive belief with absolute certainty that the Holy Quran is the seal of all Divine books and not an iota can be added to or subtracted from its prescribed teachings, inhibitions, commands and injunctions. There will be no revelation or word from God which may amend or abrogate or change or alter any of the injunctions of the Holy Quran. If anyone subscribes to such views, in our opinion, he ceases to belong to the body of believers and becomes an infidel thereby.

(Izala e Auham: Roohani Khaza'in Vol. 3:, p. 170)

51ـ اور ہم اس بات پر ایمان لاتے ہیں کہ خدا تعالیٰ کے سوا کوئی معبود نہیں اور سیّدنا حضرت محمد مصطفیٰ صلی اللہ علیہ وسلم اُس کے رسول اور خاتم الانبیاء ہیں ۔ اور ہم ایمان لاتے ہیں کہ ملائک حق اور حشرِ اجساد حق اور روزِ حساب حق اور جنت حق اور جہنّم حق ہے ۔ اور ہم ایمان لاتے ہیں کہ جو کچھ اللہ جلّ شانُہ نے قرآن شریف میں فرمایا ہے اور جو کچھ ہمارے نبی صلی اللہ علیہ وسلم نے فرمایا ہے وہ سب بلحاظ بیان مذکورہ بالا حق ہے ۔ اور ہم ایمان لاتے ہیں کہ جو شخص اس شریعتِ اسلام میں سے ایک ذرّہ کم کرے یا ایک ذرّہ زیادہ کرے یا ترکِ فرائض اور اباحت کی بنیاد ڈالے وہ بے ایمان اور اسلام سے برگشتہ ہے ۔ اور ہم اپنی جماعت کو نصیحت کرتے ہیں کہ وہ سچے دل سے اس کلمہ طیبّہ پر ایمان رکھیں کہ لَآ اِلٰهَ اِلَّا اللّٰہُ مُحَمَّدٌ رَّسُوۡلُ اللّٰہِ اور اسی پر مریں ۔ اور تمام انبیاء اور تمام کتابیں جن کی سچائی قرآن شریف سے ثابت ہے اُن سب پر ایمان لاویں ۔ اور صوم اور صلوٰۃ اور زکوٰۃ اور حج اور خدا تعالیٰ اور اس کے رسول کے مقرر کردہ تمام فرائض کو فرائض سمجھ کر اور تمام مَنہِیّات کو مَنہِیّات سمجھ کر ٹھیک ٹھیک اسلام پر کاربند ہوں ۔ غرض وہ تمام امور جن پر سلف صالحین کا اعتقادی اور عملی طور پر اجماع تھا اور وہ امور جو اہل سنّت کی اجماعی رائے سے اسلام کہلاتے ہیں اُن

62

51-We do believe that there is none worthy of worship except God Almighty and Sayyedena Hadhrat Muhammad, the Chosen One, may peace and blessings of Allah be upon him, is His Messenger and the Khatamul Anbiya. We believe that angels are a reality, that Resurrection is a reality and the Day of Judgement is a reality; that Heaven is reality and so is Hell. We do believe that whatever the Glorious and Majestic God has stated in the Holy Quran and whatever our Prophet, may peace and blessings of Allah be upon him, has stated is all, according to the aforementioned statement, the truth. We do believe that the person who subtracts an iota from the Islamic law or adds to it as much, or lays the foundation in any manner for rejection of Islamic injunctions, or attempts to declare unlawful what has been made lawful in Islam, is an infidel and a renegade to Islam. We admonish our Jamaat that they must adhere tenaciously to the fundamental article of Islamic faith.

لَآ اِلٰه اِلَّا اللّٰهُ مُحَمَّدٌ رَّسُوْلُ اللّٰهِ

"There is no God but Allah, Muhammad is His Messenger" as long as they live and that they should die holding fast to the same belief. Also they must have firm faith in all the Messengers of Allah and revealed Books which have been authenticated by the Holy Quran. They should abide strictly by the Quranic injunctions. They should strictly observe Prayers and Fast, pay Zakat and perform the Haj (pilgrimage). They should observe Islam by fully complying with all the injunctions, obligations and prohibitions pronounced by God and His Messenger. In short, all such matters, be they beliefs or deeds, on which there was

consensus of opinion among our righteous predecessors and
as are understood to be Islam by the general consensus of
opinion of those who follow the traditions of the Holy
Prophet of Islam, may peace and blessings of Allah be upon
him, should be complied with as being obligatory. We call
to witness the Heaven and the Earth, that exactly is our
Faith."

(Ayyamus Sulh, 1st Edition: Roohani Khaza'in Vol. 14, p 323)

۵۲ـاے تمام وہ لوگو جو زمین پر رہتے ہو! اور اے تمام وہ انسانی روح جو مشرق اور مغرب
میں آباد ہو! مَیں پورے زور کے ساتھ آپ کو اس طرف دعوت کرتا ہوں کہ اب زمین
پر سچا مذہب صرف اسلام ہے اور سچا خدا بھی وہی خدا ہے جو قرآن نے بیان کیا ہے۔
اور ہمیشہ کی روحانی زندگی والا نبی اور جلال اور تقدّس کے تخت پر بیٹھنے والا حضرت محمد
مصطفیٰ صلی اللہ علیہ وسلم ہے۔ (تریاق القلوب، روحانی خزائن جلد 15 صفحہ 141)

52-O ye who inhabit the earth! And O ye human spirits who
dwell in the East or in the West! I invite you most earnestly
to accept the fact that the only true faith today in the. world
is Islam and that the True God is that God who has been
mentioned in the Holy Quran, and that Prophet who
possesses eternal spiritual life the one who sits on the
throne of glory and purity is the Holy Prophet Muhammad,
the chosen one, may peace and blessings of Allah be upon him.

(Tiryaq ul Qulub: Roohani Khaza'in Vol. 15, p. 141)

ANGELS

53۔قرآن شریف پر بدیدہ تعمّق غور کرنے سے معلوم ہوتا ہے کہ انسان بلکہ جمیع کائنات الارض کی تربیت ظاہری و باطنی کے لئے بعض وسائط کا ہونا ضروری ہے اور بعض بعض اشارات قرآنیہ سے نہایت صفائی سے معلوم ہوتا ہے کہ بعض وہ نفوس طیّبہ جو ملائک سے موسوم ہیں اُن کے تعلقات طبقات سماویہ سے الگ الگ ہیں ۔بعض اپنی تاثیرات خاصہ سے ہوا کے چلانے والے اور بعض مینہ کے برسانے والے اور بعض بعض اور تاثیرات کو زمین پر اتارنے والے ہیں ۔

(توضیح مرام،روحانی خزائن جلد 3 صفحہ 70)

53-One learns from a deeper study of the Holy Quran that not only for the education and upbringing of man but also for the overt and covert progressive development of the entire universe, some intermediaries are essential between God and His creation. There are clear indications in the Holy Quran leading one to believe that the holy beings known as angels have specific relationships with various heavenly bodies. Some of them, with their special faculties, govern the phenomenon of the motion of winds and some cause rain to fall. Similarly there are others who are deputed to cause some other cosmic influences to descend upon earth.

(Tauzeeh e Maram: Roohani Khaza'in Vol. 3, p. 70)

54۔ یہ بھی یاد رکھنا چاہئے کہ اسلامی شریعت کے رو سے خواص ملائک کا درجہ خواص بشر سے کچھ زیادہ نہیں بلکہ خواص الناس ،خواص الملائک سے افضل ہیں اور نظام جسمانی

یا نظامِ روحانی میں ان کا وسائط قرار پانا اُن کی افضلیت پر دلالت نہیں کرتا بلکہ قرآن شریف کی ہدایت کے رُو سے وہ خدام کی طرح اس کام میں لگائے گئے ہیں۔

(توضیح مرام، روحانی خزائن جلد 3 صفحہ 74)

54- It should be remembered that according to Islam, angels do not possess faculties superior in rank to those possessed by human beings. For them to be granted the role of intermediaries in the physical or spiritual world does not in itself indicate their superiority. According to the Holy Quran they are assigned these functions like servants.

(Tauzeeh e Maram: Roohani Khaza'in Vol. 3, p. 74)

55- فرشتوں کا اُترنا کیا معنی رکھتا ہے۔ سو واضح ہو کہ عادت اللہ اِس طرح پر جاری ہے کہ جب کوئی رسول یا نبی یا محدَّث اصلاحِ خلقُ اللہ کے لئے آسمان سے اُترتا ہے تو ضرور اس کے ساتھ اور اس کے ہمرکاب ایسے فرشتے اُترا کرتے ہیں کہ جو مستعد دلوں میں ہدایت ڈالتے ہیں اور نیکی کی رغبت دلاتے ہیں اور برابر اُترتے رہتے ہیں جب تک کفر و ضلالت کی ظلمت دُور ہو کر ایمان اور راستبازی کی صبح صادق نمودار ہو جیسا کہ اللہ جلَّ شانہٗ فرماتا ہے۔ تَنَزَّلُ الْمَلٰئِکَۃُ وَالرُّوْحُ فِیْہَا بِاِذْنِ رَبِّھِمْ مِنْ کُلِّ اَمْرٍ سَلٰمٌ ھِیَ حَتّٰی مَطْلَعِ الْفَجْرِ (سورۃ القدر: 6-5) سو ملائکہ اور روح القدس کا تنزّل یعنی آسمان سے اُترنا اُسی وقت ہوتا ہے جب ایک عظیم الشان آدمی خلعتِ خلافت پہن کر اور کلامِ اِلٰہی سے شرف پا کر زمین پر نزول فرماتا ہے۔ روح القدس خاص طور پر اس خلیفہ کو ملتی ہے۔

(فتح اسلام حاشیہ، روحانی خزائن جلد 3 صفحہ 12)

55- What is meant by the descent of angels, one might wonder! So let it be known that according to the established ways of God, when a Messenger or a Prophet or a Muhaddith descends from heaven to reform mankind, with him invariably descend such angels as sow the seed of guidance in receptive hearts. They make them inclined towards goodness. They keep on descending until the darkness of ignorance and infidelity is dispelled by the dawn of a new day of faith and righteousness. The Holy Quran speaks of this in the verses: 'Therein descend angels and the Spirit by the command of their Lord with decrees of their Lord concerning every matter. It is all peace, till the break of dawn'. (97:5 6)

The descent of the angels and the Holy Spirit takes place when a man of outstanding qualities wearing the robe of vicegerency of God, having been blessed with Word of God, descends to earth. The Holy Spirit is especially bestowed on to him.   *(Fath e Islam: Roohani Khaza'in Vol. 3, footnote p. 12)*

REVELATION

۵۶۔ جب خدائے تعالیٰ اپنے بندہ کو کسی امرِ غیبی پر بعد دعا بندہ کے یا خود بخود مطلع کرنا چاہتا ہے تو یکدفعہ ایک بیہوشی اور ربودگی اس پر طاری کر دیتا ہے جس سے وہ بالکل اپنی ہستی سے کھویا جاتا ہے اور ایسا اس بے خودی اور ربودگی اور بیہوشی میں ڈوبتا ہے جیسے کوئی پانی میں غوطہ مارتا ہے اور نیچے پانی کے چلا جاتا ہے۔ غرض جب بندہ اس حالت ربودگی سے کہ جو غوطہ سے بہت ہی مشابہ ہے باہر آتا ہے تو اپنے اندر میں کچھ ایسا مشاہدہ کرتا ہے جیسے ایک گونج پڑی ہوئی ہوتی ہے۔ اور جب وہ گونج کچھ فرو ہوتی ہے تو ناگہاں اس کو اپنے اندر سے ایک موزون اور لطیف اور لذیذ کلام محسوس ہو جاتی ہے اور یہ غوطہ ربودگی کا ایک نہایت عجیب امر ہے جس کے عجائبات بیان کرنے کے لئے الفاظ کفایت نہیں کرتے۔ یہی حالت ہے جس سے ایک دریا معرفت کا انسان پر کھل جاتا ہے۔ کیونکہ جب بار بار دعا کرنے کے وقت خداوند تعالیٰ اس حالت غوطہ اور ربودگی کو اپنے بندہ پر وارد کر کے اس کی ہر ایک دعا کا اس کو ایک لطیف اور لذیذ کلام میں جواب دیتا ہے اور ہر ایک استفسار کی حالت میں وہ حقائق اس پر کھولتا ہے جن کا کھلنا انسان کی طاقت سے باہر ہے تو یہ امر اس کے لئے موجب مزید معرفت اور باعثِ عرفان کامل ہو جاتا ہے۔ بندہ کا دعا کرنا اور خدا کا اپنی اُلوہیت کی تجلی سے ہر ایک دعا کا جواب دینا یہ ایک ایسا امر ہے کہ گویا اسی عالم میں بندہ اپنے خدا کو دیکھ لیتا ہے اور دونوں عالم اس کے لئے بلا تفاوت یکساں ہو جاتے ہیں۔

(براہین احمدیہ حاشیہ در حاشیہ، روحانی خزائن جلد ۱ صفحہ ۲۶۰ تا ۲۶۲)

56-When God Almighty intends to inform His servant of a matter

"

pertaining to the realm of the Unknown, whether He does it in response to His servant's prayer or on His own, He brings down upon him a sort of unconsciousness and all of a sudden he loses touch with his surroundings. In that state, he completely loses awareness of even his own existence. Like a diver who plunges down to the bottom of a pool, he is completely submerged and drowned in that state of selflessness, unawareness and unconsciousness. When, in the end, he breaks surface like a diver with whom he shares his experience to a large degree and is delivered from that state of unawareness, he becomes conscious of a resonance within him. As that resonance fades out, he becomes aware of the presence of a most pleasant, well balanced and exquisite communication within him. And this experience is so strange and sublime that it is beyond one's power to describe it in words. It is this experience which reveals to one the existence of a flowing river of inner wisdom. It is through this experience of near unconsciousness that a servant of God receives from God, answers to all his supplications in an extremely exquisite and pleasant tone. Then, in response to whatever question takes shape in that state of semi unconsciousness, God reveals to him such profound knowledge as is impossible for a man to discover otherwise. This in itself results in his gaining greater faith in God and a better understanding of His wondrous ways. Man's supplication and God's response to it by way of manifestation of His being the true object of worship is an experience which enables man to behold God, as if he were seeing Him in this very world; thus be begins to belong to both worlds simultaneously.

(Braheen e Ahmadiyya: Roohani Khaza'in Vol. 1, footnote pp. 260 -262)

57۔صورتِ پنجم الہام کی وہ ہے جس کا انسان کے قلب سے کچھ تعلق نہیں بلکہ ایک خارج سے آواز آتی ہے اور یہ آواز ایسی معلوم ہوتی ہے جیسے ایک پردہ کے پیچھے سے کوئی آدمی بولتا ہے۔ مگر یہ آواز نہایت لذیذ اور شگفتہ اور کسی قدر سرعت کے ساتھ ہوتی ہے اور دل کو اس سے ایک لذت پہنچتی ہے۔ انسان کسی قدر استغراق میں ہوتا ہے کہ یکدفعہ یہ آواز آ جاتی ہے اور آواز سن کر وہ حیران رہ جاتا ہے کہ کہاں سے یہ آواز آئی اور کس نے مجھ سے کلام کی اور حیرت زدہ کی طرح آگے پیچھے دیکھتا ہے پھر سمجھ جاتا ہے کہ کسی فرشتہ نے یہ آواز دی۔ اور یہ آواز خارجی اکثر اس حالت میں بطور بشارت آتی ہے کہ جب انسان کسی معاملہ میں نہایت متفکّر اور مغموم ہوتا ہے۔

(براہین احمدیہ حاشیہ در حاشیہ،روحانی خزائن جلد 1 صفحہ 287)

57-In another type of revelation which has nothing to do with the subjective experience of the heart, one hears a voice from without as if someone were speaking from behind a curtain. This voice is very pleasing and cheerful and flows at a somewhat brisk pace fillings one's heart with ecstasy. A man's mind may have been occupied in deep thought when all of a sudden this voice is heard. Having heard this voice he is left wondering where it came from and who it was who addressed him. He looks to and fro like a surprised person and then he begins to realize that the voice had proceeded from an angel. This external voice is often heard and carries a glad tiding at a time when someone has been excessively worried and laden with grief concerning some problem.

(Braheen-e-Ahmadiyya: Roohani Khaza'in Vol. 1, footnote p. 287)

58۔یہی قانون ہے کہ جس کے پاس کچھ نور ہے اسی کو اور نور بھی دیا جاتا ہے۔ اور جس

کے پاس کچھ نہیں اس کو کچھ نہیں دیا جاتا۔ جو شخص آنکھوں کا نور رکھتا ہے وہی آفتاب کا نور پاتا ہے اور جس کے پاس آنکھوں کا نور نہیں وہ آفتاب کے نور سے بھی بے بہرہ رہتا ہے اور جس کو فطرتی نور کم ملا ہے اُس کو دوسرا نور بھی کم ہی ملتا ہے اور جس کو فطرتی نور زیادہ ملا ہے اُس کو دوسرا نور بھی زیادہ ہی ملتا ہے۔

(براہین احمدیہ حاشیہ، روحانی خزائن جلد 1 صفحہ 196،195)

58-It is so decreed that one who has a measure of light will be further enlightened. And the one who has nothing is given nothing. And one who is enlightened with the faculty of sight is the one who benefits from the light of the sun. Likewise the one who does not possess the light of eyesight remains incapable of seeing the light of the sun. Verily, a person who is less enlightened within, is also less enlightened from without. The one who is provided more abundantly with internal light will also benefit more abundantly from external light.

(Braheen-e-Ahmadiyya: Roohani Khaza'in Vol. 1, footnote pp. 195-196)

59۔ خدائے تعالیٰ نے اپنے عجیب عالم کو تین حصہ پر منقسم کر رکھا ہے۔

(1) عالم ظاہر جو آنکھوں اور کانوں اور دیگر حواس ظاہری کے ذریعہ اور آلات خارجی کے توسّل سے محسوس ہو سکتا ہے۔

(2) عالم باطن جو عقل اور قیاس کے ذریعہ سے سمجھ میں آ سکتا ہے۔

(3) عالم باطن در باطن جو ایسا نازک اور لاید رک و فوق الخیالات عالم ہے جو تھوڑے ہیں جو اس سے خبر رکھتے ہیں۔ وہ عالم غیب محض ہے جس تک پہنچنے کے لئے عقلوں کو طاقت نہیں دی گئی مگر ظن محض۔ اور اس عالم پر کشف اور روحی اور الہام کے ذریعہ سے اطلاع ملتی ہے نہ اور کسی ذریعہ سے اور جیسی عادت اللہ بدیہی طور پر ثابت اور متحقق اور متیقن

ہے کہ اس نے ان دو پہلے عالموں کے دریافت کرنے کے لئے جن کا اوپر ذکر ہو چکا ہے انسان کو طرح طرح کے حواس و قوتیں عنایت کی ہیں۔ اسی طرح اس تیسرے عالم کے دریافت کرنے کے لئے بھی اُس فیّاضِ مطلق نے انسان کے لئے ایک ذریعہ رکھا ہے اور وہ ذریعہ وحی اور الہام اور کشف ہے جو کسی زمانہ میں بکلّی بند اور موقوف نہیں رہ سکتا بلکہ اس کے شرائط بجالانے والے ہمیشہ اس کو پاتے رہے ہیں اور ہمیشہ پاتے رہیں گے۔

(سرمہ چشم آریہ، روحانی خزائن جلد 2 صفحہ 127-128 حاشیہ)

59-God Almighty has divided His wonderful universe into three categories. First, the world which is manifest and can be conceived through the eyes and the ears and other sensory organs, directly or indirectly with the help of instruments.

Secondly, the world which is hidden and which can be understood through deductive reasoning and hypothesizing.

Thirdly, the world which lies even farther than the hidden world, so hard to conceive and almost beyond the reach of imagination. Very few are those who are aware of its existence. That is an entirely obscure world which cannot be conceived through deduction but is only imagined. One can have access to it only with the help of spiritual vision or revelation or a word from God and not by any other means. As is evident from the unchanging Will of God, manifested in nature, one can safely deduce that as God has provided man with the apparatus to understand the first two categories of His creation mentioned above, similarly He must have provided man with the apparatus and instruments to conceive that world of His creation which is mentioned under the third category. And that apparatus (as we have already mentioned) comprises spiritual vision, revelation and the word of God. This mode of communication can never be conceived to be inoperative or to have ceased altogether in any age. Nay, but those who fulfilled the pre requisite have always been gifted with this and will continue to be gifted with the same.

(Surma Chashm e Arya: Roohani Khaza'in Vol. 2, p. 127-128)

THE SOUL

60۔غور سے معلوم ہوتا ہے کہ روح کی ماں جسم ہی ہے۔حاملہ عورتوں کے پیٹ میں روح کبھی اوپر سے نہیں گرتی بلکہ وہ ایک نور ہے جونطفہ میں ہی پوشیدہ طور پر مخفی ہوتا ہے اور جسم کی نشو ونما کے ساتھ چمکتا جاتا ہے۔خدائے تعالیٰ کا پاک کلام ہمیں سمجھاتا ہے کہ روح اس قالب میں سے ہی ظہور پذیر ہوجاتی ہے جونطفہ سے رحم میں تیار ہوتا ہے۔جیسا کہ وہ قرآن شریف میں فرماتا ہے۔ثُمَّ اَنْشَاْنَاهُ خَلْقًا آخَر فَتَبَارَکَ اللّٰهُ اَحْسَنُ الْخَالِقِیْنَ (سورۃ المومنون:15) یعنی پھر ہم اس جسم کو جو رحم میں تیار ہوا تھا ایک اور پیدائش کے رنگ میں لاتے ہیں اور ایک اَور خِلقت اُس کی ظاہر کرتے ہیں جو روح کے نام سے موسوم ہے اور خدا بہت برکتوں والا ہے اور ایسا خالق ہے جو کوئی اس کے برابر نہیں۔

(اسلامی اصول کی فلاسفی،روحانی خزائن جلد10 صفحہ 321)

60-Investigation reveals that the body is the mother of the soul. The soul does not fall unto the womb of a pregnant woman from on high. Instead, it is a sort of light which lies inherent in the seminal fluid which begins to shine forth along with the physical development of the foetus. The holy revelations of God help us understand that the soul is generated in the embryonic mass which begins to take shape from the seminal fluid in the uterus. As He states in the Holy Quran:

$$ثُمَّ اَنْشَاْنَاهُ خَلْقًا آخَر فَتَبَارَکَ اللّٰهُ اَحْسَنُ الْخَالِقِیْنَ$$

(Ch.23:15)

This means that then We transform the body, which was prepared in the uterus, into a new creation and evolve from it a new form of existence, which is referred to as the soul. Indeed,

God is the source of many blessings and is such a Creator as there is none like unto Him.

(Islami Usul ki Filasfi: Roohani Khaza'in Vol. 1, p. 321)

۶۱۔ جیسا کہ کوئی باغ بغیر پانی کے سرسبز نہیں رہ سکتا ایسا ہی کوئی ایمان بغیر نیک کاموں کے زندہ ایمان نہیں کہلا سکتا۔ اگر ایمان ہو اور اعمال نہ ہوں تو وہ ایمان ہیچ ہے۔ اور اگر اعمال ہوں اور ایمان نہ ہو تو وہ اعمال ریا کاری ہیں۔ اسلامی بہشت کی یہی حقیقت ہے کہ وہ اس دنیا کے ایمان اور عمل کا ایک ظلّ ہے۔ وہ کوئی نئی چیز نہیں جو باہر سے آ کر انسان کو ملے گی بلکہ انسان کی بہشت انسان کے اندر ہی سے نکلتی ہے۔ اور ہر ایک کی بہشت اسی کا ایمان اور اسی کے اعمال صالحہ ہیں جن کی اسی دنیا میں لذّت شروع ہو جاتی ہے۔ (اسلامی اصول کی فلاسفی، روحانی خزائن جلد ۱۰ صفحہ ۳۹۰)

As no garden can flourish without water, no faith can be considered live without good deeds. It is meaningless to have faith without righteous actions; likewise good deeds without faith are a vain display. According to Islam, heaven in fact is the reflected image of our faith and good deeds. It is not something new which will be delivered to man from outside. In fact it is created from within him. Each man's heaven is born out of his own faith and good deeds, which he begins to experience and enjoy in this very life.

(Islami Usul ki Filasfi: Roohani Khaza'in Vol. 10, p. 390)

LIFE AFTER DEATH

۔62 اسلام میں یہ نہایت اعلیٰ درجہ کی فلاسفی ہے کہ ہر ایک کو قبر میں ہی ایسا جسم مل جاتا ہے کہ جو لذّت اور عذاب کے ادراک کرنے کے لئے ضروری ہوتا ہے۔ ہم ٹھیک ٹھیک نہیں کہہ سکتے کہ وہ جسم کس مادہ سے طیّار ہوتا ہے کیونکہ یہ فانی جسم تو کالعدم ہو جاتا ہے اور نہ کوئی مشاہدہ کرتا ہے کہ در حقیقت یہی جسم قبر میں زندہ ہوتا ہے اس لئے کہ بسا اوقات یہ جسم جلایا بھی جاتا ہے اور عجائب گھروں میں لاشیں بھی رکھی جاتی ہیں اور مدتوں تک قبر سے باہر بھی رکھا جاتا ہے۔ اگر یہی جسم زندہ ہو جایا کرتا تو البتہ لوگ اس کو دیکھتے مگر باایں ہمہ قرآن سے زندہ ہو جانا ثابت ہے لہٰذا یہ ماننا پڑتا ہے کہ کسی اور جسم کے ذریعہ سے جس کو ہم نہیں دیکھتے انسان کو زندہ کیا جاتا ہے اور غالباً وہ جسم اسی جسم کے لطائف جوہر سے بنتا ہے تب جسم ملنے کے بعد انسانی قویٰ بحال ہوتے ہیں۔ اور یہ دوسرا جسم چونکہ پہلے جسم کی نسبت نہایت لطیف ہوتا ہے اس لئے اس پر مکاشفات کا دروازہ نہایت وسیع طور پر کھلتا ہے۔

(کتاب البریہ، روحانی خزائن جلد 13 صفحہ 71-70)

62-Islam expounds the most excellent doctrine that in the interim period after death, every soul is vested with a sort of body which is essential for perception of pleasure and torment. We cannot accurately describe as to what substance that body is made of. As far as this mortal body is concerned, however, it ceases to exist. Moreover, it is never observed by anyone that the same corporal body is revived in the grave. On the contrary, this body is often cremated, and many a time corpses are also preserved in museums, or kept otherwise out of the grave for long periods. If it were the same body which were to be revived, it was very likely that people would have observed this happening. Nonetheless, the revival of the dead is very much evident from the study of the Holy Quran. Hence one is compelled to believe that the dead are revived in such forms as we cannot see. Most likely that spiritual body is composed of some highly refined constituents of this material body. The soul having been thus provided with a body, human perceptions are reinstated. Because this new body is far more rarefied and ethereal in nature, a much wider avenue of visions and revelation is laid open to it.

(Kitab ul Barriyya: Roohani Khaza'in Vol. 13, pp. 70-71)

SIN

63۔گناہ درحقیقت ایک ایسا زہر ہے جو اُس وقت پیدا ہوتا ہے کہ جب انسان خدا کی اطاعت اور خدا کی پرجوش محبت اور محبّا نہ یاد الٰہی سے محروم اور بے نصیب ہو۔ اور جیسا کہ ایک درخت جب زمین سے اکھڑ جائے اور پانی چوسنے کے قابل نہ رہے تو وہ دن بدن خشک ہونے لگتا ہے اور اس کی تمام سرسبزی برباد ہو جاتی ہے۔ یہی حال اُس انسان کا ہوتا ہے جس کا دل خدا کی محبت سے اکھڑا ہوا ہوتا ہے۔ پس خشکی کی طرح گناہ اس پر غلبہ کرتا ہے۔ سو اس خشکی کا علاج خدا کے قانون قدرت میں تین طور سے ہے۔ (۱) ایک محبت (۲) استغفار جس کے معنے ہیں دبانے اور ڈھانکنے کی خواہش۔ کیونکہ جب تک مٹی میں درخت کی جڑ جمی رہے تب تک وہ سرسبزی کا امیدوار ہوتا ہے۔ (۳) تیسرا علاج توبہ ہے۔ یعنی زندگی کا پانی کھینچنے کے لئے تذلّل کے ساتھ خدا کی طرف پھرنا اور اس سے اپنے تئیں نزدیک کرنا اور معصیت کے حجاب سے اعمال صالحہ کے ساتھ اپنے تئیں باہر نکالنا۔ اور توبہ صرف زبان سے نہیں ہے بلکہ توبہ کا کمال اعمال صالحہ کے ساتھ ہے۔ تمام نیکیاں توبہ کی تکمیل کے لئے ہیں۔

(سراج الدین عیسائی کے چار سوالوں کا جواب، روحانی خزائن جلد 12 صفحہ 328۔329)

63-Sin, which indeed is a poison, is born when a man is wanting in obedience to God and is empty of His love and His affectionate remembrance. The fate of a man whose heart has become cold to the love of God is like that of an uprooted tree, no longer capable of drawing the sap of life from the soil. As such a tree gradually withers and dies out, so, like the dryness of the tree, sin overwhelms the heart. The remedy for this state of dryness, according to the law of nature is of three types:

(1) Love (2) Istighfar, i.e. seeking forgiveness of Allah. It literally means a desire to bury or to cover, reminding one that as long as the root of the tree is buried in the soil it can hope to bring forth green foliage. (3) The third remedy is tauba, which means to turn towards God in all humility drawing the sap of life and to bring oneself closer to Him to break loose with the help of righteous deeds from the enveloping cover of sinfulness. Tauba cannot be achieved merely by word of mouth; in fact tauba can be perfected only with the help of righteous deeds. All acts of goodness are aimed at achieving perfection of tauba.

(Sirajuddin Isai ke Char Sawalon ka Jawab: Roohani Khaza'in

Vol. 12, p 328-329)

SALVATION

۶۴۔ وہ مسئلہ جو انجیل میں نجات کے بارہ میں بیان کیا گیا ہے یعنی حضرت عیسیٰ علیہ السلام کا مصلوب ہونا اور کفّارہ، اِس تعلیم کو قرآن شریف نے قبول نہیں کیا۔ اور اگرچہ حضرت عیسیٰؑ کو قرآن شریف ایک برگزیدہ نبی مانتا ہے اور خدا کا پیارا اور مقرب اور وجیہ قرار دیتا ہے لیکن اس کو محض انسان بیان فرماتا ہے اور نجات کے لئے اس امر کو ضروری نہیں جانتا کہ ایک گناہ گار کا بوجھ کسی بے گناہ پر ڈال دیا جائے۔ اور عقل بھی تسلیم نہیں کرتی کہ گناہ تو زید کرے اور بکر پکڑا جائے۔ اس مسئلہ پر تو انسانی گورنمنٹوں نے بھی عمل نہیں کیا۔ افسوس کہ نجات کے بارہ میں جیسا کہ عیسائی صاحبوں نے غلطی کی ہے ایسا ہی آریہ صاحبوں نے بھی اس غلطی سے حصہ لیا ہے اور اصل حقیقت کو بھول گئے ہیں کیونکہ آریہ صاحبان کے عقیدہ کی رُو سے توبہ اور استغفار کچھ بھی چیز نہیں اور جب تک انسان ایک گناہ کے عوض وہ تمام جُونیں نہ بھگت لے جو اس گناہ کی سزا مقررہ ہے تب تک نجات غیر ممکن ہے۔

(چشمۂ معرفت، روحانی خزائن جلد 23 صفحہ 414)

64-The doctrine of salvation [that atonement can be achieved through the crucifiction of Jesus, peace be upon him] as set out in the Gospels, is rejected by the Holy Quran. Despite the fact that the Holy Quran affirms Jesus to be a noble prophet of God and declares him to be very dear to Him, and describes him to be noble and dignified in bearing, he is presented as a mere human being. Also, the Holy Quran does not admit in principle, the concept that for the sake of atonement, the burden of a sinful person can be transferred to another innocent being. Likewise human logic does not accept the notion either, that for the sin of Tom, Dick should be indicted. Even worldly governments have never subscribed to this notion. Alas, as far as the concept of atonement is concerned, the Aryas have also committed the same mistake as has been committed by the Christians. They too have missed the mark. According to the Arya doctrine, both repentance and seeking forgiveness are utterly meaningless. Reincarnation being the prescribed punishment in Arya doctrine, they believe that unless a person is subjected to various reincarnations for having committed even a single crime, atonement is simply impossible.

(Chashma e Marifat: Roohani Khaza'in Vol. 23, p. 414)

PRAYERS

۵۶۔''جب اللہ تعالیٰ کافضل قریب آتا ہے تو وہ دعا کی قبولیت کے اسباب بہم پہنچا دیتا ہے۔ دل میں ایک رقّت اور سوز و گداز پیدا ہوجاتا ہے۔ لیکن جب دعا کی قبولیت کا وقت نہیں ہوتا تو دل میں اطمینان اور رجوع پیدانہیں ہوتا۔طبیعت پر کتنا ہی زور ڈالو مگر طبیعت متوجہ نہیں ہوتی۔اس کی وجہ یہ ہے کہ کبھی خدا تعالیٰ اپنی قضا وقدر منوانا چاہتا ہے اور کبھی دعا قبول کرتا ہے اس لئے میں تو جب تک اِذن الٰہی کے آثار نہ پالوں قبولیت کی کم امید کرتا ہوں اور اس کی قضا وقدر پر اس سے زیادہ خوشی کے ساتھ جو قبولیت دعا میں ہوتی ہے راضی ہوجاتا ہوں کیونکہ اس رضا بالقضا کے ثمرات اور برکات اس سے بہت زیادہ ہیں''۔ (ملفوظات جلد اوّل صفحہ 304 ۔ایڈیشن 2003ء)

65-When the blessings of Allah are near at hand, He provides the pre-requisites for the acceptance of prayer. The heart is stirred, warms up and begins to glow. When, however, the moment is not opportune for the acceptance of prayer, the heart lacks that tranquillity which results in turning towards God. However much one exerts one's self, the heart does not respond by exhibiting willingness. It is so because at times God exerts His decree so that His Will be done, and at other times He concedes to the prayer of His servants.

That is why as long as I do not perceive the signs of God's willingness, I do not entertain much hope for the acceptance of prayer. At such times, I submit to the Will of my Lord with greater pleasure than that which I derive from the acceptance of prayer. Indeed, I know that the blessings and fruits of this submission to the Will of God are greater by far.

(Malfoozat Vol. 1: p 304, edition 2003)

JIHAD

(Striving in the Cause of Allah)

۶۶۔ اسلام نے کبھی جبر کا مسئلہ نہیں سکھایا۔ اگر قرآن شریف اور تمام حدیث کی کتابوں اور تاریخ کی کتابوں کو غور سے دیکھا جائے اور جہاں تک انسان کے لئے ممکن ہے تدبّر سے پڑھا یا سنا جائے تو اس قدر وسعتِ معلومات کے بعد قطعی یقین کے ساتھ معلوم ہوگا کہ یہ اعتراض کہ گویا اسلام نے دین کو جبراً پھیلانے کے لئے تلوار اٹھائی ہے نہایت بے بنیاد اور قابلِ شرم الزام ہے اور یہ ان لوگوں کا خیال ہے جنہوں نے تعصّب سے الگ ہو کر قرآن اور حدیث اور اسلام کی معتبر تاریخوں کو نہیں دیکھا بلکہ جھوٹ اور بہتان لگانے سے پورا پورا کام لیا ہے۔ مگر میں جانتا ہوں کہ اب وہ زمانہ قریب آتا جاتا ہے کہ راستی کے بھوکے اور پیاسے ان بہتانوں کی حقیقت پر مطلع ہو جائیں گے۔ کیا اُس مذہب کو ہم جبر کا مذہب کہہ سکتے ہیں جس کی کتاب قرآن میں صاف طور پر یہ ہدایت ہے کہ لَاۤ اِکۡرَاہَ فِی الدِّیۡنِ (سورۃالبقرۃ:253) یعنی دین میں داخل کرنے کے لئے جبر جائز نہیں۔ کیا ہم اُس بزرگ نبی کو جبر کا الزام دے سکتے ہیں جس نے مکّہ معظّمہ کے تیرہ برس میں اپنے تمام دوستوں کو دن رات یہی نصیحت دی کہ شر کا مقابلہ مت کرو اور صبر کرتے رہو۔ ہاں جب دشمنوں کی بدی حد سے گزر گئی اور دین اسلام کے مٹا دینے کے لئے تمام قوموں نے کوشش کی تو اس وقت غیرتِ الہّی نے تقاضا کیا کہ جو لوگ تلوار اٹھاتے ہیں وہ تلوار ہی سے قتل کئے جائیں۔ ورنہ قرآن شریف نے ہرگز جبر کی تعلیم نہیں دی۔ اگر جبر کی تعلیم ہوتی تو ہمارے نبی صلی اللہ علیہ وسلم کے اصحاب جبر کی تعلیم کی وجہ سے اس لائق نہ ہوتے کہ امتحانوں کے موقع پر سچے ایمانداروں کی طرح صدق دکھلا سکتے۔ لیکن ہمارے سیدّ و مولّیٰ نبی

صلی اللہ کے صحابہ کی وفاداری ایک ایسا امر ہے کہ اس کے اظہار کی ہمیں ضرورت نہیں۔ یہ بات کسی پر پوشیدہ نہیں کہ ان سے صدق اور وفاداری کے نمونے اس درجہ پر ظہور میں آئے کہ دوسری قوموں میں ان کی نظیر ملنا مشکل ہے۔ اس وفادار قوم نے تلواروں کے نیچے بھی اپنی وفاداری اور صدق کو نہیں چھوڑا بلکہ اپنے بزرگ اور پاک نبی کی رفاقت میں وہ صدق دکھلا یا کہ کبھی انسان میں وہ صدق نہیں آ سکتا جب تک ایمان سے اس کا دل اور سینہ منور نہ ہو۔ غرض اسلام میں جبر کو دخل نہیں ۔

(مسیح ہندوستان میں، روحانی خزائن جلد 15 صفحہ 11ـ12)

66-Islam never advocated compulsion. If the Holy Quran, the books of Hadith and historical records are carefully examined and as far as possible, studied and listened to attentively, one is bound to reach the positive conclusion that the allegation that Islam permitted the use of sword for the spread of religion is shameless and utterly unfounded. This in fact, is the view held by only those who have not studied the Holy Quran or the Traditions or other reliable sources of Islamic history without prejudice. Not only this but some have even gone to the extent of fabricating lies and levying unfounded charges without inhibition. I know that the time is approaching fast when those who are hungry and thirsty for Truth will see through their deception. Can a religion be described as a religion of compulsion when its Holy Book, the Quran, has categorically prohibited the use of force for the spread of faith? So says the Holy Quran:

لَا اِكْرَاہَ فِی الدِّیْنِ

'There is no compulsion in religion.' (Ch.2:256)

Can we accuse that great Prophet of using force against others, who, for thirteen years, day and night, exhorted all his Companions in Mecca not to return evil for evil but forbear and forgive? When however, the mischief of the enemy exceeded all limits and when all the various peoples around him made determined efforts to exterminate Islam, God's attribute that He always defends His beloved ones so demanded:

'Let those who raised the sword perish by the sword.'

Otherwise in no way has the Holy Quran permitted compulsion in religion. If compulsion in any way had been employed in winning converts and the Companions of our Holy Prophet had been the fruit of compulsion, it would have been impossible for them to have demonstrated: at the time of trials, such steadfastness and sincerity as only true believers can display. The loyalty and faithfulness of the Companions of our Master, the Holy Prophet (peace be on him) is a fact so well known as need no comment from us. It is no secret that among them are examples of loyalty and steadfastness the parallel of which is difficult to find in the annals of other nations; this body of the faithful did not waver in their loyalty and steadfastness even under brandishing swords. On the contrary, in the company of their Great and Holy Prophet, may peace and blessings of Allah be upon him, they displayed such steadfastness which no man can demonstrate unless his heart and his bosom are lit up with the light of faith. Hence compulsion had no role to play in Islam.

(Masih Hindustan Mein: Roohani Khaza'in, Vol. 15, pp. 11-12)

67۔ تمام سچے مسلمان جو دنیا میں گزرے کبھی بھی اُن کا یہ عقیدہ نہیں ہوا کہ اسلام کو تلوار سے پھیلانا چاہئے بلکہ ہمیشہ اسلام اپنی ذاتی خوبیوں کی وجہ سے دُنیا میں پھیلا ہے۔ پس جو لوگ مسلمان کہلا کر صرف یہی بات جانتے ہیں کہ اسلام کو تلوار سے پھیلانا چاہئے وہ اسلام کی ذاتی خوبیوں کے معترف نہیں ہیں۔

(تریاق القلوب حاشیہ، روحانی خزائن جلد 15 صفحہ 167)

67-None of the true Muslims who ever lived maintained that force should be employed in the spread of Islam. On the other hand, Islam has always flourished on the strength of its inherent qualities of excellence. Those who having the distinction of being called Muslims, yet believe that Islam should be spread with force, do not seem to have any awareness of the inherent beauties of Islam.

(Tiryaqul Qulub: Roohani Khaza'in Vol. 15, footnote, p 167)

KINDNESS UNTO MANKIND

68۔ہمارا یہ اصول ہے کہ کل بنی نوع کی ہمدردی کرو۔ اگر ایک شخص ایک ہمسایہ ہندو کو دیکھتا ہے کہ اس کے گھر میں آگ لگ گئی اور یہ نہیں اٹھتا کہ تا آگ بجھانے میں مدد دے تو مَیں سچ سچ کہتا ہوں کہ وہ مجھ سے نہیں ہے۔ اگر ایک شخص ہمارے مریدوں میں سے دیکھتا ہے کہ ایک عیسائی کو کوئی قتل کرتا ہے اور وہ اس کے چھڑانے کیلئے مدد نہیں کرتا تو مَیں تمہیں بالکل درست کہتا ہوں کہ وہ ہم میں سے نہیں ہے۔

(سراج منیر، روحانی خزائن جلد 12 صفحہ 28)

68-The principle to which we adhere is that we have kindness at heart for the whole of mankind. If anyone sees the house of a Hindu neighbour on fire and does not come forward to help extinguish the fire, most truly I declare that he does not belong to me. If anyone of my followers, having seen someone attempting to murder a Christian does not endeavour to save him, I most truly declare that he does not belong to us.

(Siraj e Muneer: Roohani Khaza'in Vol. 12, p 28)

69۔مَیں تمام مسلمانوں اور عیسائیوں اور ہندوؤں اور آریوں پر یہ بات ظاہر کرتا ہوں کہ دنیا میں کوئی میرا دشمن نہیں ہے۔ مَیں بنی نوع سے ایسی محبت کرتا ہوں کہ جیسے والدہ مہربان اپنے بچوں سے بلکہ اُس سے بڑھ کر۔ میں صرف اُن باطل عقائد کا دشمن ہوں جن سے سچائی کا خون ہوتا ہے۔ انسان کی ہمدردی میرا فرض ہے اور جھوٹ اور شرک اور ظلم اور ہر ایک بد عملی اور نا انصافی اور بد اخلاقی سے بیزاری میرا اصول ۔

(اربعین نمبر 1، روحانی خزائن جلد 17 صفحہ 344)

69-I proclaim to all Muslims, Christians, Hindus and Aryas, that I have no enemy in the world. I love mankind with the love that a compassionate mother has for her children; even more so. I am only the enemy of the false doctrines which kill truth. Human sympathy is my duty. My principle is to discard falsehood. I reject paganism, wrongdoing, misconduct, injustice and immorality.

(Arbaeen, Pt. 1: Roohani Khaza'in, Vol. 17, p. 344)

THE TRUE NATURE OF GOG AND MAGOG

۷۰۔ یاجوج ماجوج وہ قوم ہے جو تمام قوموں سے زیادہ دنیا میں آگ سے کام لینے میں استاد بلکہ اس کام کی موجد ہے۔ اور ان ناموں میں یہ اشارہ ہے کہ اُن کے جہاز، اُن کی ریلیں، اُن کی کلیں آگ کے ذریعہ سے چلیں گی اور اُن کی لڑائیاں آگ کے ساتھ ہوں گی اور وہ آگ سے خدمت لینے کے فن میں تمام دنیا کی قوموں سے فائق ہوں گے اور اِسی وجہ سے وہ یاجوج ماجوج کہلائیں گے۔ سو وہ یورپ کی قومیں ہیں جو آگ کے فنون میں ایسے ماہر اور چابک اور یکتائے روزگار ہیں کہ کچھ بھی ضرور نہیں کہ اس میں زیادہ بیان کیا جائے۔ پہلی کتابوں میں بھی جو بنی اسرائیل کے نبیوں کو دی گئیں یورپ کے لوگوں کو ہی یاجوج ماجوج ٹھہرایا ہے بلکہ ماسکو کا نام بھی لکھا ہے جو قدیم پایۂ تخت روس تھا۔ سو مقرر ہو چکا تھا کہ مسیح موعود یاجوج ماجوج کے وقت میں ظاہر ہوگا۔ (ایام الصلح، روحانی خزائن جلد ۱۴ صفحہ ۴۲۴۔۴۲۵)

70-Gog and Magog are a people who surpass all others in their ability to put fire to various uses and are indeed pioneers in this field. Their very names (Note: in Arabic Yajooj and Majooj are derived from the word ajeej which means fire) indicate that all their inventions, be they ships, trains or other machines, were to be fuelled with fire. And they would fight their battles with firearms. They would excel all other nations on the earth in pressing fire into their service. This is why they are called Yajooj and Majooj. Obviously, therefore, they are the European nations who in the science of utilizing fire are so skilful, adept and outstanding that it needs not be elaborated upon. They are the same Europeans who have been referred to as Gog and

Magog in the old scriptures given to the Israelite prophets. Moscow is even mentioned therein by name, which was the capital of ancient Russia. It was destined that the Promised Messiah would appear in the age of Gog and Magog.

(Ayyamus Sulk Roohani Khaza'in Vol. 14, p 424-425)

SEASON OF LIGHT

۷۱۔جیسا کہ تم دیکھتے ہو کہ پھل اپنے وقت پر آتے ہیں ایسا ہی نور بھی اپنے وقت پر ہی اترتا ہے۔اور قبل اس کے جو وہ خود اترے کوئی اس کو اتار نہیں سکتا۔اور جبکہ وہ اترے تو کوئی اس کو بند نہیں کرسکتا۔مگر ضرور ہے کہ جھگڑے ہوں اور اختلاف ہو مگر آخر سچائی کی فتح ہے۔کیونکہ یہ امر انسان سے نہیں ہے اور نہ کسی آدم زاد کے ہاتھوں سے بلکہ اُس خدا کی طرف سے ہے جو موسموں کو بدلاتا اور وقتوں کو پھیرتا اور دن سے رات اور رات سے دن نکالتا ہے۔وہ تاریکی بھی پیدا کرتا ہے مگر چاہتا روشنی کو ہے۔وہ شرک کو بھی پھیلنے دیتا ہے مگر پیار اس کا توحید سے ہی ہے اور نہیں چاہتا کہ اس کا جلال دوسرے کو دیا جائے۔جب سے کہ انسان پیدا ہوا ہے اُس وقت تک کہ نابود ہو جائے خدا کا قانون قدرت یہی ہے کہ وہ توحید کی ہمیشہ حمایت کرتا ہے۔

(مسیح ہندوستان میں، روحانی خزائن جلد 15 صفحہ 65)

71-As you observe the fruit to appear in season, so also the Light descends at its appointed time; none can cause it to descend before; it comes of its own accord, nor can one obstruct its passage when it begins to descend. There will be disputes and controversies, but at the end Truth must prevail. It is so because this is not the work of man nor is it within the power of the children of Adam. It is the work of Almighty God Who rotates the seasons, changes times, and brings forth the day from the night and the night from the day. Though He creates darkness as well, it is the light which He really desires. He also permits idolatry to spread, yet it is Unity which He loves to see prosper. He does not will that His majesty be shared by others. Ever since man came to be born, until the time that he ceases to be, it is the unchanging law that God will remain on the side of Unity (belief in the Oneness of God). (Masih Hindustan Mein: Roohani Khaza'in, Vol. 15, p 65)

72۔ اے خدا اے کارساز و عیب پوش و کردگار

اے مرے پیارے مرے محسن مرے پروردگار

یہ سراسر فضل و احساں ہے کہ مَیں آیا پسند

ورنہ درگہ میں تیری کچھ کم نہ تھے خدمت گزار

دوستی کا دم جو بھرتے تھے وہ سب دشمن ہوئے

پر نہ چھوڑا ساتھ تُو نے اے مرے حاجت برار

اے مرے یارِ یگانہ اے مری جاں کی پنہ

بس ہے تُو میرے لئے مجھ کو نہیں تجھ بن بکار

میں تو مر کر خاک ہوتا گر نہ ہوتا تیرا لطف

پھر خدا جانے کہاں یہ پھینک دی جاتی غبار

اے فدا ہو تیری راہ میں میرا جسم و جان و دل

مَیں نہیں پاتا کہ تجھ سا کوئی کرتا ہو پیار

ابتدا سے تیرے ہی سایہ میں میرے دن کٹے

گود میں تیری رہا میں مثلِ طفلِ شیر خوار

نسلِ انساں میں نہیں دیکھی وفا جو تجھ میں ہے

تیرے بن دیکھا نہیں کوئی بھی یارِ غمگسار

لوگ کہتے ہیں کہ نالائق نہیں ہوتا قبول

مَیں تو نالائق بھی ہو کر پاگیا درگہ میں بار

اِس قدر مجھ پر ہوئیں تیری عنایات و کرم

جن کا مشکل ہے کہ تا روزِ قیامت ہو شمار

(براہین احمدیہ حصہ پنجم، روحانی خزائن جلد 21 صفحہ 127)

72-O God,

O Maker of things;
Who protects me from being exposed;
Thou art the Provident,
O my Beloved,
my Benefactor, my Sustainer.

It is sheerly
out of grace;
that Thou hast chosen me;
Otherwise there was no dearth
of servants in Your court.

Those who
used to profess friendship
turned into enemies;
But Thou hast
never abandoned me;
O friend in need.

O beloved
Who has no equal,
the refuge of my life;
Sufficient for me are You
without You I am nought.
But for Your kindness,

I would have turned to dust;
Then how and where
that dust is thrown away
only Allah knows.

O how I yearn
that in Your path,
my life, My body and my heart
be sacrificed.
I don't see how anyone could ever love like You do.

I have spent my early days,
under Your benign shadow.
You carried me in Your lap
like a suckling infant.
I never witnessed such fidelity
in the human race,
as You possess.
There does not exist a friend,
who can commiserate like Thee.

They say that none
is accepted without merit.
Lo, being without merit,
I have been granted
a station in Thy court.

You have overwhelmed me
with such favour and kindness
as cannot be recounted
Till the end of time.

(Braheen e Ahmadiyya, Pt. V: Roohani Khaza'in Vol. 21, p 127)

WORLD RELIGIONS

73۔منجملہ اُن اصولوں کے جن پر مجھے قائم کیا گیا ہے ایک یہ ہے کہ خدا نے مجھے اطلاع دی ہے کہ دنیا میں جس قدر نبیوں کی معرفت مذہب پھیل گئے ہیں اور استحکام پکڑ گئے ہیں اور ایک حصّۂ دنیا پر محیط ہو گئے ہیں اور ایک عمر پا گئے ہیں اور ایک زمانہ ان پر گزر گیا ہے ان میں سے کوئی مذہب بھی اپنی اصلیت کے رُو سے جھوٹا نہیں اور نہ ان نبیوں میں سے کوئی نبی جھوٹا ہے۔

(تحفہ قیصریہ، روحانی خزائن جلد 12 صفحہ 256)

73-Of all the principles to which I have been made to adhere firmly, there is one that has specifically been revealed to me by God Himself. That principle is to desist from declaring false in essence, such religions as have been revealed by God through His prophets and which have the following characteristics. They have met with wide acceptance in certain regions of the world; having survived all challenges, they have become well established and deeply rooted. Having stood the test of time for long, they have acquired a measure of age and an air of permanence. According to this principle, such religions are essentially true and their founders were most certainly true prophets of God.

(Tohfa Qaisariya: Roohani Khaza'in Vol. 12, p 256)

74۔یہ اصول نہایت پیارا اور امن بخش اور صلح کاری کی بنیاد ڈالنے والا اور اخلاقی حالتوں کو مدد دینے والا ہے کہ ہم اُن تمام نبیوں کو سچا سمجھ لیں جو دنیا میں آئے۔ خواہ ہند میں ظاہر ہوئے یا فارس میں یا چین میں یا کسی اور ملک میں اور خدا نے کروڑہا دلوں میں ان کی عزت اور

(تحفہ قیصریہ،روحانی خزائن جلد12 صفحہ 259)

74-This is a most attractive and peace giving principle which provides the basis for reconciliation amongst nations and promotes better moral conduct. This principle teaches us to believe in the truth of all prophets wherever they might have appeared; in India, Persia or China or any other country and for whom God has filled the hearts of millions of people with awe and deep respect and has caused their religions to be firmly rooted.

(Tohfa Qaisariya: Roohani Khaza'in Vol. 12, p 259)

THE FUTURE OF AHMADIYYAT

۷۵۔ مَیں بڑے دعوے اور استقلال سے کہتا ہوں کہ مَیں سچ پر ہوں اور خدائے تعالٰی کے فضل سے اِس میدان میں میری ہی فتح ہے اور جہاں تک مَیں دُور بین نظر سے کام لیتا ہوں تمام دنیا اپنی سچائی کے تحتِ اقدام دیکھتا ہوں اور قریب ہے کہ مَیں ایک عظیم الشان فتح پاؤں کیونکہ میری زبان کی تائید میں ایک اور زبان بول رہی ہے اور میرے ہاتھ کی تقویت کے لئے ایک اَور ہاتھ چل رہا ہے جس کو دنیا نہیں دیکھتی مگر میں دیکھ رہا ہوں۔ میرے اندر ایک آسمانی روح بول رہی ہے جو میرے لفظ اور حرف حرف کو زندگی بخشتی ہے۔ اور آسمان پر ایک جوش اور اُبال پیدا ہوا ہے جس نے ایک پُتلی کی طرح اس مُشتِ خاک کو کھڑا کر دیا ہے۔ ہر ایک وہ شخص جس پر توبہ کا دروازہ بند نہیں عنقریب دیکھ لے گا کہ مَیں اپنی طرف سے نہیں ہوں۔ کیا وہ آنکھیں بینا ہیں جو صادق کو شناخت نہیں کر سکتیں؟ کیا وہ بھی زندہ ہے جس کو اس آسمانی صدا کا احساس نہیں؟

(ازالہ اوہام، روحانی خزائن جلد 3 صفحہ 403)

75-I declare with full confidence and steadfastness that I am in the right and that with the Grace of Allah, I will emerge victorious in this struggle. As far as I can observe with my far-reaching sight, I see the entire world ultimately covered by the advancing step of my truth. The time is near at hand before I shall gain a resounding victory. It is so because another voice speaks in support of what I speak and there is another Hand which operates to strengthen my hand. This is not perceived by the world but I see it. In me vibrates the voice of a heavenly spirit which instils each word I speak with life. There is commotion and upsurge in heaven which has fashioned out of a handful of dust, a puppet figure whose movements are manipulated from on high. All those upon whom the door of repentance is not yet closed will soon see that I am not of my own accord. Can they be seeing with eyes which fail to recognize a man of truth? Can he be deemed alive who has no awareness of this Heavenly call.

(Izalah Auham Pt. II: Roohani Khaza'in Vol. 3, p 403)

76-Rest assured that this is a tree planted by the Hand of God. He will never permit it to go to waste. He will not be satisfied until He has seen it through to its fullness. He will see to it that it is well irrigated and will build a protective fence around it. Thus God will bless my followers with astounding progress and prosperity. Have you left any stones unturned? Had it been the work of man, this tree would have been cut and felled since long and no trace of it would have remained.

(Anjaam e Atham: Roohani Khaza'in Vol. 11, p 64)

ULTIMATE VICTORY

۷۷ـ زمین کے لوگ خیال کرتے ہوں گے کہ شاید انجام کار عیسائی مذہب دنیا میں پھیل جائے یا بدھ مذہب تمام دنیا پر حاوی ہو جائے مگر وہ اِس خیال میں غلطی پر ہیں ۔ یاد رہے کہ زمین پر کوئی بات ظہور میں نہیں آتی جب تک وہ بات آسمان پر قرار نہ پائے ۔ سو آسمان کا خدا مجھے بتلاتا ہے کہ آخر کار اسلام کا مذہب دلوں کو فتح کرے گا۔

(براہین احمدیہ حصہ پنجم ، روحانی خزائن جلد 21 صفحہ 427)

77-People of the world may be inclined to think that it is Christianity which may ultimately spread throughout the world, or it may be Buddhism which will prevail in the end. But they are certainly wrong in these conjectures. Remember that nothing happens on this Earth unless it has been so willed in Heaven. And, it is the God of Heaven who revealed to me that ultimately it will be the religion of Islam which will conquer the hearts of people.

(Braheen e Ahmadiyya, Pt. 5: Roohani Khaza'in Vol. 21, p 427)

www.ingramcontent.com/pod-product-compliance
Lightning Source LLC
LaVergne TN
LVHW020910200726